The 24 hours of Le Mans

David Taylor

Clink
Street

Published by Clink Street Publishing 2023

Copyright © 2023

First edition.

The author asserts the moral right under the Copyright, Designs and Patents Act 1988 to be identified as the author of this work.

ISBN:
978-1-915229-80-9 - paperback
978-1-915229-91-5 - hardback
978-1-915229-81-6 - ebook

With thanks to…

*My Mum for her time, help and endless encouragement.
To my Grandparents, especially my Granddad, his love of books
and motor racing has been a massive influence on me, and to all
my family and friends for their love and support.*

FAME
PRESTIGE
LE MANS
1923
NIGHT
PORSCHE
MONEY INOVATION
ACCOMPLISHMENT
EXCITEMENT
RIVALRY
DEVELOPMENT
SPEED
ENDURANCE
FERRARI
FRANCE
PROTOTYPE SPORTS CAR
HISTORY

WELCOME

Hello and welcome to an illustrated history of the 24 hours of Le Mans – the most prestigious automobile race in the world. In 2023 the French classic celebrates its 100th year since the inaugural race back in 1923. This book will cover the great cars, the great drivers, the historic track, the highs and lows and so much more.

Le Mans 24 hours. The story so far

AN APPETITE FOR SPEED

THE VERY BEGINNING

The very first car was invented by Karl Benz back in 1886. The car was known as the "Benz Patent-Motorwagen" and only had three wheels. The motorcar had room for two people and had a top speed of ten miles per hour. The automobile was seen as an alternative to the horse and people quickly wanted to see how fast it could go.

In 1894, thousands of people gathered in northern France to watch a trial to publicise the motor car. It was an 80-mile drive from Paris to Rouen and back. The winner would be judged if the car "was easy to handle, without danger and cheap to run." Twenty-one cars started and seventeen finished. Officially the event was not a race, but everyone there wanted to know who was the fastest. The unofficial winner was Count Albert de Dion driving his "steam tractor" averaging 11.6 mph. The trial was an enormous success, and de Dion organised a race from Paris to Bordeaux and back for the following year, the fastest car would be the winner. This was truly the moment when motorsport was born.

In 1895 the first ever official motor race took place – the Paris–Bordeaux–Paris. The rules were simple: cars had to carry two or more people and could be driven by more than one driver. There was also a time limit of 100 hours. The race spanned 11–13 June 1895. Twenty-one cars started, eleven made it to Bordeaux and nine made it back. French driver Émile Levassor was first to arrive, after 732 miles with a total time of 48 hours and 48 minutes. But because the car was a two-seater, it was ineligible for first prize. So, Paul Koechlin driving a Peugeot was named as the winner and received the main prize. Koechlin averaged 12.2 mph over the 732 miles.

On 28 November, the *Chicago Times-Herald* race took place in America. The prize money was $5,000, approximately $160,000 in today's money. This was a race to help promote the motorcar and the first in the United States. The winner of the 57-mile race was Karl Benz in his own car.

After this, Grand Prix racing became more popular, and the sport began to grow. However not everyone favoured car racing – some said it was too dangerous. To prove them wrong, the Grand Prix of Endurance was created to show cars were safe over a long period of time. This race would take place at Le Mans in France.

THE FIRST LE MANS

1923

After the growth of Grand Prix racing – and the interest from France – the Automobile Club de l'Ouest (ACO) launched the Grand Prix of Endurance and the inaugural race took place in 1923. This is what we now know as the 24 hours of Le Mans. Categories for the race were decided by engine size, a total of four classes were created. Thirty-seven cars started the race from twenty different manufacturers. Eighteen of those being French with one Bentley representing Great Britain and two Excelsior cars entered from Belgium. Each car would have two drivers, doing roughly two-hour stints before swapping over. The track – the Circuit de la Sarthe – had previously been used for the 1906 French Grand Prix and was approximately ten miles long. It ran from the outskirts of Le Mans city; it ran on the main road southwards to the village of Mulsanne and back. The race began at 4 pm on the 26th May 1923, shortly after a hailstorm. Of the thirty-seven starters, thirty finished with Chenard-Walcker cars coming first and second. French drivers André Lagache and René Léonard won the race and the whole event was a massive success.

LA COUPE
RUDGE-WHITWORTH

CIRCUIT DE LA SARTHE

TRACK GUIDE

Length: 8.467 Miles

Turns: 38

Race Lap Record: 3:17.297 Mike Conway driving the Toyota TS050 Hybrid in 2019

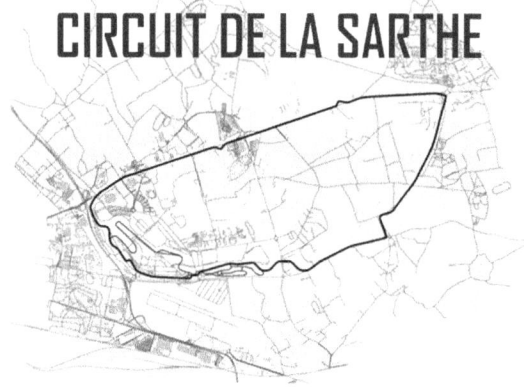

 Circuit de La Sarthe is one of the most iconic circuits in the world. It is also unique as half the track is permanently a race facility and part public road. The course is also one of the longest still being used today, a total of 8.467 miles being the current length. The permanent track is called the Bugatti Circuit, which in 1967 hosted the French Grand Prix. Circuit de la Sarthe turns off at turn two of the Bugatti track and sweeps through the Esses section. It re-joins at the last corner of the track through a chicane, whereas the Bugatti circuit ends with a double-apex hairpin.

Circuit de la Sarthe is a demanding track on man and machine, as 85% of the lap is on full throttle but certain corners like Mulsanne

Corner and Arnage prove to be punishing on the brakes. Also, due to half the track being public road, there are various changes of surface making it ultimate test for any car and driver. Before two chicanes were added on the 3.7-mile long Mulsanne Straight in 1990, a top speed of 251 mph was set by the Peugeot in 1988.

Circuit de la Sarthe was first used for the French Grand Prix in 1906 and since then the track has changed multiple times becoming the circuit it is today.

PIT LANE

The pits at Le Mans have developed with the track over time. The start/finish straight and pit lane began with some small pit garages which gradually has become a two-storey building with roof terrace. In 1971 a pit wall was added, it was simply just one piece of Armco splitting the track from the pits. It stayed this way for some time until an entirely new complex along the front stretch was built, housing modern pit boxes, garages, and an observation suite above the garages. Now the pit lane is full with sixty-two garages ensuring Le Mans will continue to have a packed grid.

DUNLOP CURVE

The Dunlop Curve is the first corner of the lap and is a fast right-hand bend. The corner has got tighter over time, mainly because of the chicane that was introduced in 1987.

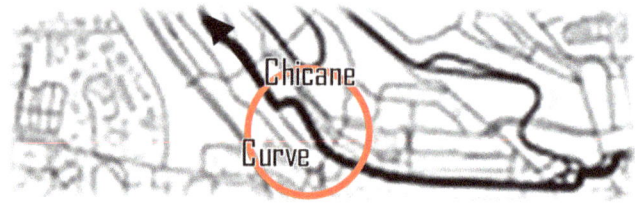

DUNLOP CHICANE

The Dunlop Chicane is the first hard braking point on the track, and it is a left then right going downhill under the Dunlop Bridge towards the Esses. The Dunlop Bridge is in the shape of a giant tyre and is a Le Mans landmark, and it is also a footbridge.

ESSES

One of the most challenging sections of the track, the Esses, are a slightly banked quick complex of corners. Before 2002, there was just one corner known as the Esses leading onto Tertre Rouge.

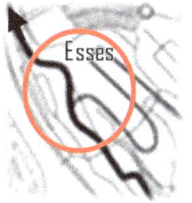

TERTRE ROUGE

Arguably the most famous corner on the track – Tertre Rouge, is a nearly flat-out bend that leads onto the Mulsanne Straight. Tertre Rouge corner is named after the colour of the surrounding soil. The corner links the racetrack to the public road.

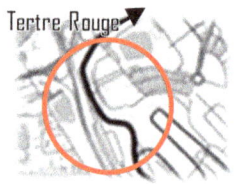

MULSANNE STRAIGHT

The Mulsanne Straight is 3.7 miles, one of the longest straights in the motorsport world. The straight starts at the exit of Tertre Rouge where it is important for drivers to get a good exit, because if not it can compromise your speed down the long straight. This long straight has proved to be a suitable place for pushing a car to the limit. The fastest speed recorded during a race was 251 mph, this was in 1988 driven by Roger Dorchy in his Peugeot P88. Due to the safety concern after many tragic accidents, in 1990 two chicanes were added to help keep speeds down. When races are not taking place, the Mulsanne Straight is public road, the first part of the Circuit de la Sarthe which is not permanent race facility. It is called the Ligne droite des Hunaudières, which leads to the town of Mulsanne.

MULSANNE CORNER

Mulsanne Corner is one of the most demanding turns on the Le Mans circuit due to the harsh work on the brakes through the entire race. At the end of one of the longest fastest straights is the toughest braking point on the track. Next to the little town of Mulsanne, the right-angle corner leads back onto another very fast section of track. Mulsanne corner can make or break a race, particularly in the early morning when cold brakes and misty weather can lead to unusual mistakes.

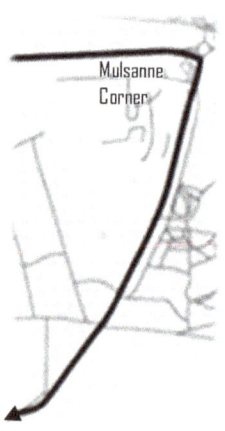

SIGNALLING PIT

The old signalling pit is located on the exit of Mulsanne corner. Due to modern in-car radio technology, the signalling area does not exist anymore. However, in the days before a driver could communicate to the team by radio, he would use hand signals and a man would phone the team saying what the problem was. This system also worked in reverse, if the team wanted a driver to make a pitstop, a phone call was made from the pits and message would go out on a pit board from the signalling pits.

FROM MULSANNE CORNER TO INDIANAPOLIS

This section of track does not have an official name, however it is one of the fastest sections of the track. A series of blind crests and a gradual turn to the right can prove challenging, especially in the early evening as the sun goes down and is at eye line.

INDIANAPOLIS

Formally known as the Arnage Esses, Indianapolis is a banked corner, just like the racetrack in America. A 90° left bend is a slow corner and underneath are 3.2 million bricks – some from Indianapolis motor speedway – to give the corner its steep shape.

ARNAGE

Arnage is the slowest corner on the track. It is where a good qualifying lap can be lost, with not much opportunity to gain time. Situated near the end of the road section of track, Arnage is named after a local village.

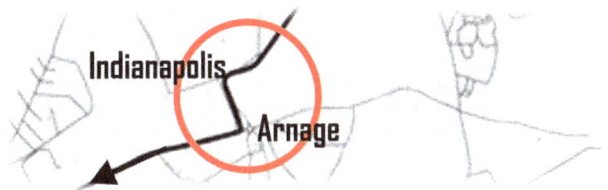

FROM ARNAGE TO THE PORSCHE CURVES

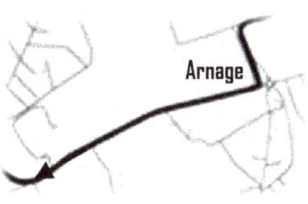

Similar to the section from Mulsanne corner to Indian-apolis, this part of track has no official name. It is one of the fastest sections of track, a few brisk curves and the last part of public road. This is also one of the narrowest sections of track – just the two lanes. The next sweeping right bend turns onto permanent racetrack known as the Porsche curves.

PORSCHE CURVES

The Porsche Curves are one of the most demanding sections on the modern Le Mans track. Previously the complex was one fast-left hand corner which led onto the start/finish straight but has gradually developed into a fast sequence of corners similar to the Esses. A car with high downforce will benefit in the Porsche curves as well as a driver with oodles of bravery!

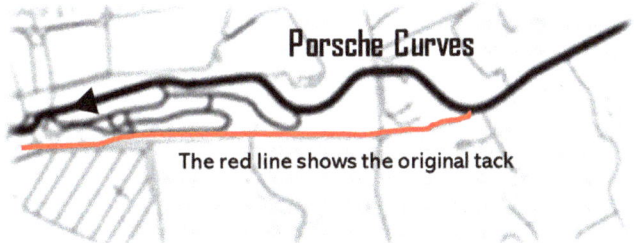

The red line shows the original tack

FORD CHICANE

Similar to the Porsche Curves, the Ford Chicane was once just a straight road leading back to the start/finish line. Now it is a sequence of tight corners in quick succession. The first curves of the complex were built in 1968 and was paid for by Ford, hence the name. As the Porsche Curves developed, the Ford Chicane had to as well, which has become the Chicane we have today. Also, the entrance to pit lane is now a chicane too.

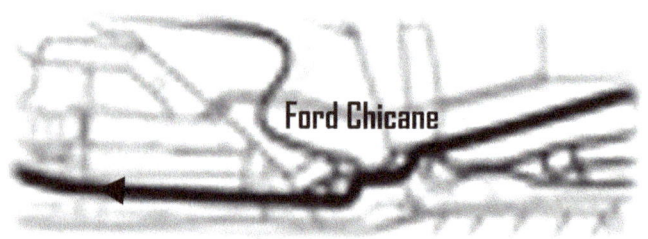

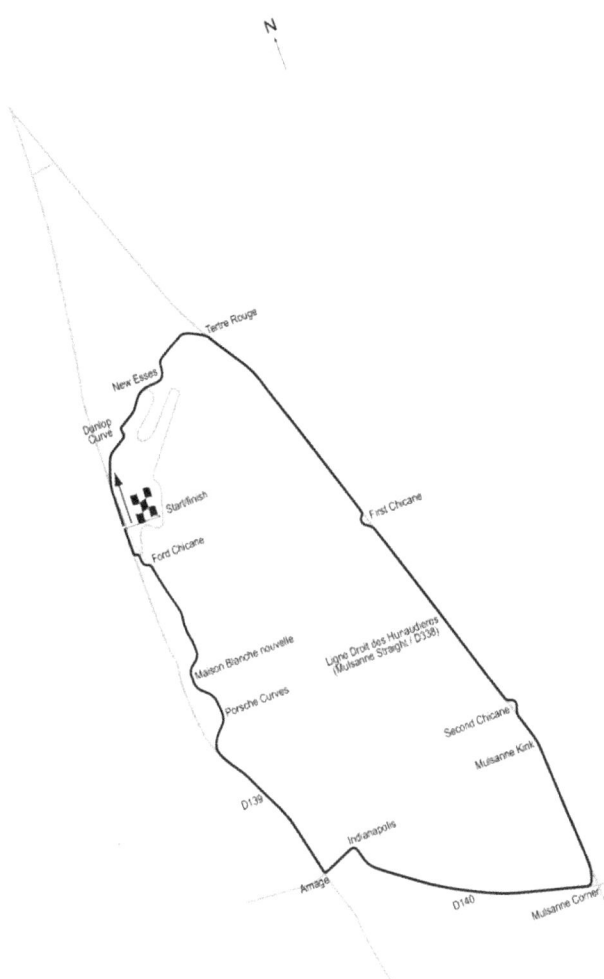

LAP RECORDS

Over the 100-year history of Le Mans, the track has evolved and changed. These are the lap records for each layout

Years	Circuit length	Lap record in race
1923–1928	10.726 miles	8:07 (79.289 mph) in 1928 Tim Birkin in a Bentley
1929–1931	10.153 miles	6:48 (89.702 mph) in 1930 Tim Birkin in a Bentley
1932–1955	8.384 miles	4:06.6 (122.387 mph) in 1955 Mike Hawthorn in a Jaguar D Type
1956–1967	8.364 miles	3:23.6 (147.895 mph) in 1967 Mario Andretti and Denny Hulme in a Ford Mk IV
1968–1971	8.369 miles	3:18.4 (151.861 mph) in 1971 Jakie Oliver in a Porsche 917
1972–1978	8.476 miles	3:34.2 (142.446 mph) in 1978 Jean-Pierre Jabouille in an Alpine-Renault A443
1979–1985	8.467 miles	3:25.1 (148.613 mph) in 1985 Jaky Ickx in a Porsche 962
1986	8.406 miles	3:23.3 (148.850 mph) in 1986 Klaus Ludwig in a Porsche 956
1987–1989	8.410 miles	3:21.27 (150.430 mph) in 1989 Alain Ferté in a Jaguar XJR9
1990–1996	8.451 miles	3:27.47 (146.635 mph) in 1993 Eddie Irvine in a Toyota TS010
1997–2001	8.454 miles	3:35.032 (141.530 mph) in 1999 Ukyo Katayama in a Toyota GT-One
2002–2005	8.482 miles	3:33.483 (143.028 mph) in 2002 Tom Kritstensen in an Audi R8
2006	8.482 miles	3:31.211 (144.567 mph) in 2006 Tom Kristensen in an Audi R10 TDI
2007–2017	8.469 miles	3:17.475 (154.385 mph) in 2015 André Lotterer in an Audi R18 e-tron quattro
Since 2018	8.467 miles	3:17.297 (154.5 mph) in 2019 Mike Conway in a Toyota TS050

THE FIRST YEARS

1924–1939

In 1924, Bentley entered a full factory team and, as Excelsior pulled out of the race, they became the only non-French team to enter the race. From the start of the race, 1923 winners André Lagache and René Léonard in the Chenard-Walcker took an early lead for the opening hours. Unfortunately, after 3 hours the French car caught fire putting them out of the race. After this, a fierce battle developed between the Lorraine-Dietrich team and the Bentley. After 6 hours there were only twenty-five of the forty-one starters still running. The Bentley driven by John Duff made an unscheduled pitstop, with a blocked gearbox and they had to spend half an hour in the pits. This put the Lorraine-Dietrich team into first and second by midnight but soon after the Bentley had caught them up. This battle raged on until the leader skated off the road, which damaged the chassis. The car was able to continue after spending a while in the pits. This left the second Lorraine car in the lead dicing with the Duff-driven Bentley. But at 9 am the Lorraine got a puncture leaving the Bentley with a one lap lead, which was maintained to the finish. The "Bentley Boys" John Duff and Frank Clement took their first win at Le Mans with their three-litre sport.

In 1925 André Rossignol and Gérard de Courcelles struck back in their Lorraine-Dietrich and took victory, and the following year the French team dominated again with a 1–2–3 finish. In 1927 pre-race favourites Bentley took a second win at Le Mans, but it didn't go smoothly. The race is most famous for the White House crash, a wreck which involved eight cars including all three Bentleys. Back then the track was narrow and this incident blocked the road, yet the racing was able to continue. The crash damaged the leading Bentley driven by Dudley Benjafield and Sammy Davis but they were able to continue to win by a staggering twenty laps, the biggest gap in Le Mans history.

Bentley were still the team to beat in 1928, but a packed grid of entrants from France, Italy, America and England meant the defending champions were up against it if they wanted to defend their title. This was also a significant year because it was the first time foreign cars outnumbered French ones. However, the French teams were right up the front and the race is best known for the leading duel between French Stutz team and the British Bentleys. After 24 hours of battling the #4 Bentley took victory with Woolf Barnato and Bernard Rubin at the wheel, one lap ahead of the Stutz. 1929 was an important year for the track as a new spectator area was made between Indianapolis and Arnage helping create more publicity for the race. The "Bentley Boys" triumphed again with a dominant 1–2–3–4 result, the first time that had been achieved in Le Mans history. The race was one of the toughest yet, with only ten cars making it to the finish line.

1929 results

Pos	No	Team	Drivers	Chassis
1	1	Bentley Motors Ltd	Woolf Barnato *Sir* Henry "Tim" Birkin	Bentley Speed Six
2	9	Bentley Motors Ltd	Glen Kidston Jack Dunfee	Bentley 4½ Litre

Pos	No	Team	Drivers	Chassis
3	10	Bentley Motors Ltd	*Dr* Dudley Benjafield *Baron* André d'Erlanger	Bentley 4½ Litre
4	8	Bentley Motors Ltd	Frank Clement Jean Chassagne	Bentley 4½ Litre

The 1930 race was once again dominated by Bentley coming first and second. Only seventeen cars started the race, the smallest grid in Le Mans history, yet the entrants were competitive. Especially

Mercedes who were keen to make an impact and pushed the Bentleys very hard. However, during the night the German car was retired with a flat battery. The Fox & Nicholl Talbot team finished third, seventeen laps off of the winning Bentley. This was to be the British team's last Le Mans victory until 2003. In 1931, after the Bentley team decided not to continue in Le Mans, the competition was wide open with Bugatti, Mercedes and Alfa Romeo all strong contenders. The private British team Earl Howe of Alfa Romeos won in a gruelling race where only six cars made it to the finish. The following year was an Italian invasion at Le Mans as the Alfa Romeo team stepped up their endurance racing programme to take a 1–2 result. The Italian team had previously had success at the 1,000-mile Mille Miglia and the 24 hours of Spa. The supercharged cars were separated by just two laps and the winner was thirty-eight laps ahead of the third placed Talbot AV105. 1933 was a significant year for the track with the long Pontlieue suburb being shortened to create a long-curved turn one, down a short hill and through a complex of corners known as the Esses. The race proved to be one of the most exciting yet.

The Alfa Romeos were still the most competitive car on the grid and a total of five privateer teams brought the Italian car to Le Mans with world competitive driver line-ups. The competition was up against it and quite soon into the practice session the Alfas were running very strongly and the race would become a battle between the Italian cars. All the opposition were European based with cars coming from Aston Martin, Amilcar, Riley, MG and Bugatti. The race started on a bright sunny day and 50,000 traveled to watch the eleventh Grand Prix of Endurance. The Bugatti teams tried to take the fight to the Alfas but the pace was huge and the race quickly developed into a race of driving skill, luck and the most efficient team/crew. By the second lap, Raymond Sommer in the leading Alfa Romeo had lapped the British Austin car. He continued to build up a lead and by the second hour he had lapped all the cars apart from the three Alfa Romeos in second, third and fourth. Having handed over to his teammate, Tazio Nuvolari put in a super stint in the evening and as this was Nuvolari's first Le Mans and it was best to leave the night driving to the experienced Sommer. After 12 hours the pair had a two-lap lead, but developed leaking fuel tank and it took 18 minutes to fix it. By the morning Nuvolari found he needed to make up 4 minutes behind Franco Cortese in the Alfa Romeo. An hour later though Nuvolari had retaken the lead and then extended it to almost a lap. As Franco Cortese tried to keep up, he crashed at Indianapolis and chassis damage put him out of the race. Nuvolari had settled into the lead but in the early afternoon the car developed a fuel leak and a series of pitstops were needed to properly fix the problem. This meant Philippe Varent in the #8 Alfa Romeo took the lead. Nuvolari struggled with fading brakes but somehow managed to close in on the leading car, with Luigi Chinetti at the wheel. With just 8 minutes to go Chinetti had to pit for a fuel top-up and came out with a slim lead. But on the final lap he missed a gear and braked too late meaning Nuvolari was able to get passed to win by just 400 metres.

Chinetti managed to put right what happened the year before and take his second Le Mans win in 1934 with Philippe Étancelin as his co-driver. The 1935 race was another tense one, decided on the last lap with the Lagonda team taking its only Le

Mans win beating the Pierre Louis-Dreyfus Alfa Romeo team. 1936 was scheduled to happen on the 14th and 15th June but due to the French going on strike there was a lack of workers to modify the streets for the race. The race took place a year later and Bugatti took their first of two Le Mans wins. In 1938 the privately entered Delahaye 135CS won the race with Bugatti winning again in 1939. By the end of the '30s, motor racing was really starting to take off and become more popular but due to the Second World War there was a ten-year hiatus until racing could continue at Le Mans.

SPORTS CAR RACING

Sports car racing, also known as Endurance or long-distance racing, is a unique form of motorsport where two, three or four drivers share a car, switching throughout the race. A predetermined distance can be covered in a set number of laps in an endurance race, or a given amount of time might be set aside for competitors to cover as much distance as they can. Most typical distances for endurance events is 1,000 km (620 m), or around 6 hours, but longer races can be 8 hours, 1,000 miles, 12 hours or 24 hours. This means racing through the night is common and sports car racing is seen as a real test of skill, bravery and determination for the teams and drivers. The Le Mans 24 hours is the oldest active endurance race.

Endurance races are often split into multiple categories or classes based on engine size or category of driver. Regulations have changed over time, but generally there are two main classes of cars, Prototype and Grand Tourers (GT). Prototype cars are usually the fastest/top class and win the race overall. The regulations for this class are often very specialised meaning teams with big budgets and lots of research and development (R&D) is needed to produce a winning car. The GT classes are based on road cars turned into racing cars, such as the Porsche 911 or Ferrari 458. This is often a very competitive class of racing and winners could be a manufacturers team or a private team. Ultimately this results in drivers aiming to win overall or their class own, but all this happens on the same racetrack at the same time. This can result in danger as cars that are going sometimes up to 70 mph quicker come up behind slower cars. The driving gets even more difficult during the night when a driver of a slower car might not see a prototype car closing in on them at a higher speed. To try and solve this problem, the FIA created a rule that all GT cars had to have yellow headlights and Prototype cars white headlights, so in the night a competitor knew which class of car was in their mirrors. This reduced the number of accidents. However, the yellow headlights not bright enough and reduced visibility, so now all cars need to have white headlights.

Another unique factor of sports car racing is that a car is shared between more than one driver. Due to the length of the race a driver would get too tired, so drivers do stints. After a shift of 2 hours a driver will bring the car into the pits, get out and another driver from his team takes over. This adds another element to this team sport with communicating to each other during the race.

The original system for defining classes was done by engine size and this system was used until the Group 5 and Group 6 regulations in the 1970s. Group 5 and Group 6 were done in a similar way with engine capacity being the main factor as well as weight and power. To some extent in the '80s Group C was similar. In the '90s LMGT1 replaced Group C and this category appealed to manufacturers because they could use heavily modified road cars or make some production-based models of the Le Mans prototype car. The hi-tech hybrid LMP1 era followed, before the current Hypercar class.

Prototype classes		
Class		**Years won at Le Mans**
3.0	/3-litre	1923, 1924, 1927, 1931, 1934,
5.0	5-litre	1925, 1926, 1928, 1932, 1933, 1935, 1937, 1938
8.0	8-litre	1929, 1939
<3.0	<3-litre	1930
S 2.0	Sports 2000	1949
S 5.0	Sports >2000	1950, 1951, 1953 – 1957
S 3.0	Sports 3000	1952, 1958 – 1961
E +3.0	Experimental 3.0	1962
P 3.0	Prototype 3000	1963
P 4.0	Prototype 4000	1964, 1965
P +5.0	Prototype >5000	1966, 1967
Gr.5	Group 5	1968 – 1975, 1979

Prototype classes		
Class		**Years won at Le Mans**
Gr.6	Group 6	1976, 1977, 1978, 1980, 1981
C	Group C	1982, 1983
C1	Group C1	1984 – 1990, 1992, 1993
C2	Group C2	1991
LMGT1	Le Mans Group GT1	1994, 1995, 1998
LMP	Le Mans Prototype	1996, 1997, 1999 – 2020
Hypercar	Le Mans Hypercar	2021 –

The Triple Crown of Motorsport is achieved if one driver wins the three most prestigious races, Le Mans 24 hours, Indianapolis 500 and the Monaco GP. This has only been achieved by Graham Hill. The Triple Crown in Endurance Racing is made up of Le Mans as well as the Sebring 12 hours and the 24 hours of Daytona. A total of nine drivers have achieved this and some others have come very close. However, no driver has won all three events in the same year. Ken Miles came the closest to doing this before he was robbed of his Le Mans victory in 1966. Another special achievement happened in 1961 when Phil Hill became the only driver to win Le Mans and the Formula 1 World Championship in the same year.

Winners of the endurance triple crown			
Driver	**24 hours of Daytona**	**12 hours of Sebring**	**24 hours of Le Mans**
Hans Herrmann	1968	1960, 1968	1970
Jackie Oliver	1971	1969	1969
Hurley Haywood	1973, 1975, 1977, 1979, 1991	1973, 1981	1977, 1983, 1994
A. J. Foyt	1983, 1985	1985	1967

Winners of the endurance triple crown			
Driver	24 hours of Daytona	12 hours of Sebring	24 hours of Le Mans
Al Holbert	1986, 1987	1976, 1981	1983, 1986, 1987
Andy Wallace	1990, 1997, 1999	1992, 1993	1988
Mauro Baldi	1998, 2002	1998	1994
Marco Werner	1995	2003, 2005, 2007	2005, 2006, 2007
Timo Bernhard	2003	2008	2010, 2017

TRADITIONS

As Le Mans is a race which dates back to 1923 it has its own unique traditions and has a famous one-of-a-kind timetable. Traditionally, the Le Mans test day would be held at the end of April but due to the pandemic the 2020 and 2021 test days were cancelled. After the 2022 race the ACO will permanently move the test day to one week before the race. The Le Mans race is usually the climax of a long exciting week. Scrutineering on Monday and Tuesday, practice/qualifying on Wednesday and Thursday before a rest day on Friday, which traditionally has no on-track action and the very popular drivers parade takes place. The race starts on Saturday and finishes on Sunday.

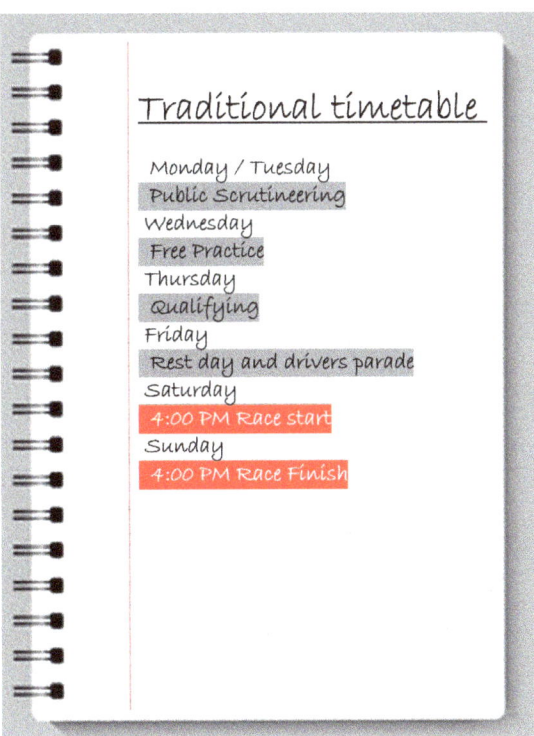

THE STARTING CEREMONY

The starting ceremony has been a tradition for many years. The winner from the previous year arrives in a historic car to return the champions trophy. Then the French national anthem 'La Marseillaise' is sung with a brass band playing on the track. The French army arrive by helicopter and fast-rope down from it to bring the tricolor flag which is used to start the race. Then French air force display team Patrouille de France perform a fly past down the start/finish straight. Every year an honorary starter is chosen to wave the tricolour to start the race.

RADIO LE MANS

Radio Le Mans was first broadcast at the 1987 24 hours of Le Mans after a successful special event broadcast the year before. The radio station is really popular and useful to help keep track of what is going on during the race. Also, various bits of commentary from Radio Le Mans have been used in movies such as *Journey to Le Mans*.

THE LE MANS START

The Le Mans Start was used from 1923 to 1969. The system was unique, the drivers line-up on one side of the track with their cars parked opposite. The official starter stood in the middle of the road holding the French flag high in the air. At 4 pm, the flag is dropped and the drivers sprint across the track, jump in, start the car, and drive off. Until 1962, the cars were lined up in order of engine capacity, but from 1963 onwards the grid had been formed by qualifying times. This became a safety issue in the late 1960s when some drivers ignored their safety harnesses, leading to drivers running the first few laps either improperly harnessed or sometimes not at all. This tragically led to several deaths. In 1969 Jackie Ickx protested the start system and the officials listened so in 1970 cars were still lined up along the pit wall, but the drivers were already inside and strapped in. At the dropping of the French tricolor, the drivers started their engines and drove away. Since 1971 a rolling start system has been used.

WALK OF FAME

The Empreintes des vainqueurs began in 1991 and has become a popular tradition. The winning drivers make their handprints in plaster which later becomes a mould for a bronze plaque. The plaques are all put on the street in the town of Le Mans and at the end of the walk of fame is a big statue of the Le Mans track.

POST-RACE TRADITIONS

Le Mans has several post-race traditions. On the final lap of the race the drivers slow down for a "photo finish" but sometimes this can be dangerous because cars might still be battling for position. On the victory lap the marshals wave all the safety flags to congratulate the drivers. When Dan Gurney won the 1967 race he began the tradition of spraying the winners champagne instead of drinking it from a glass! Before the podium ceremony, the winner drives down the pit lane in the opposite direction to usual with the two co-drivers on the roof of the winning car before parking at the victory spot.

DANGER

1949–1959

The 1950s is widely known as the most dangerous era in motorsport history. As speed increased safety was not a priority and fatal accidents were regular. 1949 was the first race to be held after the Second World War. It took four years to rebuild the infrastructure because during the war the Luftwaffe had used the pits as an airbase and the Mulsanne straight as a runway. The 1949 race was very important as it was the first time a Ferrari won the race with Luigi Chinetti and Peter Mitchell-Thomson taking victory in their private 166. Chinetti had achieved his third Le Mans win and would go on to be very important figure in private Ferrari racing. Farther and son team of Louis Rosier and Jean-Louis Rosier won in 1950, driving a Talbot-Lago T26. However, Louis didn't trust his son so he opted not to hand over during the scheduled driver changes, instead driving for a total of 23 hours and 15 minutes! The pair won by just one lap ahead of the other Talbot-Lago T26 and a British entered Cadillac rounded out the podium in third.

1951 was the first year Jaguar won at Le Mans and was the beginning of an intense period of sports car racing with Jaguar, Ferrari, Porsche and Aston Martin battling for honours. In 1952 Mercedes won with their W194 car, however the German victory was not popular at the time. Mercedes dominated with a 1–2 result and both with an all-German driver line-up raising the bar of endurance racing. In order to beat the efficient direct injection engines of the Mercedes, Jaguar developed a stronger braking system. The new Jaguar was called the C-Type and became the first car to race at Le Mans with disc brakes, which proved to be a tremendous advantage especially at Mulsanne Corner. The Jaguars came first, second and fourth with Duncan Hamilton and Tony Rolt winning. This was also the first year in Le Mans history that the winning team had averaged over 100 mph and the race was now part of the new World Sports Car Championship (WSCC). Rolt and Hamilton returned the following year with the Jaguar team, this time with an updated

D-Type model. However this year the British team faced stiff opposition from Aston Martin and Ferrari. The weather was wet throughout the majority of the race but the treacherous conditions didn't stop a fierce battle which lasted the whole race. In the end Ferrari took their second win at Le Mans, just one lap ahead of the D-Type Jaguar.

1955 was set to be one of the most competitive in Le Mans history with Juan Manuel Fangio and Stirling Moss in the lead Mercedes. Moss fresh from his Mille Miglia win was one of the favourites for victory. Defending champions Ferrari along with Aston

Martin, Maserati and Cunningham were the strong opposition for the German team, as well as Jaguar with Formula 1 driver Mike Hawthorn at the wheel of the #6 car. The race started at a furious pace with Hawthorn and Moss battling for the lead but only thirty-five laps in at 6:20 pm disaster struck. While lapping a backmarker before coming into the pits, Hawthorn swerved in front of the Austin-Healey driven by Lance Macklin. As Macklin moved over his left-rear hit the front-right of Pierre Levegh's Mercedes. The collision lead to the worst motor racing disaster in history.

This is what the *Memphis Press-Scimitar* newspaper said the Monday after:

Death Toll Reaches 79 at French Track

LE MANS, France – Two additional deaths among the injured raised the toll of auto racing's worst disaster to 79 today. Premier Edgar Faure's Government announced it would seek means of preventing a recurrence. Mass funeral services will be held in Le Mans' 600-year-old Cathedral tomorrow for the victims killed when French driver Pierre Levegh's silver Mercedes-Benz hit another sports car, soared into the air, exploded and spread death in a crowd packed 20 deep behind an earthen barrier.

After the tragedy of 1955, Mercedes pulled out of sports car racing. Stirling Moss joined Aston Martin forming a strong partnership with the team. Defending champion Mike Hawthorn returned with the Jaguar team in one of three updated D-Types. Before the 1956 race got underway, there was a minute silence to respect the events from the previous year. The race proved to be an intense battle between Aston Martin, Jaguar and Ferrari. Moss managed to perfect the Le Mans start and was the first away into the lead. Soon into the race Hawthorn had to pit with a misfire problem which would hinder him throughout the whole race. The Ferraris had issues during the night so, by the morning it was a straight fight between the Stirling Moss Aston Martin and the #4 D-Type. Annoyingly for Moss and Collins the car lost second gear in the morning, which meant Ninian Sanderson and Ron Flockhart could hold on and win in the Jaguar.

Pos	No	Team	Drivers	Chassis
1	4	Ecurie Ecosse	Ninian Sanderson Ron Flockhart	Jaguar D-Type
2	8	Aston Martin Ltd.	Stirling Moss Peter Collins	Aston Martin DB3S
3	12	Scuderia Ferrari	Olivier Gendebien Maurice Trintignant	Ferrari 625 LM

Due to the Le Mans tragedy in 1955, Le Mans was not in-cluded in the WSCC schedule for 1956 but it was reintroduced for the 1957 season. Some 250,000 spectators came to witness a five-way manufacture dule between Ferrari, Maserati, Jaguar, Aston Martin and Porsche. The weather was cloudy and unpre-dictable and before the race started the crowd were treated to a demonstration run of seventy French classic cars to celebrate fifty years of the ACO. At the start Peter Collins in the Ferrari Type 335 S lead from three Aston Martins on the first lap. But already the Ferraris were struggling, on only the second lap Col-lins had to reduce pace due to engine trouble and was forced to retire at the end of the second lap when it seized completely. This put the two Maseratis of Stirling Moss and Jean Behra in the lead. The Ferraris were still running strongly and after 2 hours, Hawthorn was leading over the two Maseratis with the army of four Jaguars closing in. Problems hit the Maseratis soon after as Moss was forced to retire with a smoking engine. The Aston Martins and Porsches were not able to challenge as much as they had hoped going to the race. As problems hit the leading Italian cars Jaguar moved into a dominant 1–2–3–4 position at the halfway stage which they maintained to the finish with Ron Flockhart and Ivor Bueb winning. Ferrari were able to finish a distant fifth, twenty-seven laps down. Scuderia Ferrari were not happy with being defeated and the Italian team created a new car called the 250 TR/58 which took advantage of rule changes for the 1958 WSCC season. The car was dominant and took victory in the opening three rounds of the WSCC, with Aston Martin winning round four. Round five of the season was Le Mans and Ferrari entered as clear favourites with three cars from the Scuderia plus two more from Luigi Chinetti's North American racing team as well as some other independent teams. David Brown Racing entered three Aston Martin DBR1 cars aiming to take the fight to Ferrari. The race was once again dominated by the wet weather conditions, but this didn't stop Stirling Moss taking an early lead in the Aston Martin, he was followed by a Jaguar and two Ferraris. Moss though was on another level and kept extending the gap at the front by 3 seconds a lap with the Ferraris working their way up into second and third places. The British Jaguars didn't have the pace to stay at the front. Moss was in control until 3 hours in when he was forced to stop with a broken conrod and he retired from the race. During the night Jaguar took the fight to the Ferraris but ultimately the Italian cars had tremendous pace meaning Phil Hill and Olivier Gendebien took victory. The one remaining Aston Martin finished second ahead of three Porsches. Having just missed out on Le Mans victory in 1958, the Aston Martin team dominated the last round of the season at Goodwood finishing 1–2–3 and claiming third in the manufacturers' championship. The British team were so confident with their DBR1, which had been raced since 1956, that they entered it again at Le Mans for the 1959 race. The problem for the Aston Martin team was that the DBR1 was less reliable than their rivals meaning Ferrari would be able to keep up a better pace throughout the race. So for the race Stirling Moss was given the job of setting a high pace to make the Ferraris drive faster than they would want to, to try and break them. This plan worked, although Moss retired, the Ferrari team all suffered with engine issues. The Aston Martin team had two cars left fighting at the front and they finished first and second. Carroll Shelby and Roy Salvadori won the gruelling race and Aston Martin went on to win the WSCC later on in the year. But the Le Mans victory was tougher than it seemed especially for Shelby. The fantastic American driver had suffered from a heart condition from the age of four. During the 1959 Le Mans Shelby's heart condition had got increasingly worse and he suffered several small heart attacks. Somehow he was able to continue driving and take victory but after the 1960 season he quit driving and set up Shelby American race team.

Aston Martin DBR1 pictured at Sebring

1959 Results

Pos	No	Team	Drivers	Chassis
1	5	David Brown Racing	Carroll Shelby Roy Salvadori	Aston Martin DBR1/300
2	6	David Brown Racing	Maurice Trintignant Paul Frère	Aston Martin DBR1/300
3	11	Equipe Nationale Belge	Jean Blaton Leon Dernier	Ferrari 250 GT LWB
4	18	North American Racing Team	George Arents André Pilette	Ferrari 250 GT LWB
5	16	F. Tavano *(private entrant)*	Fernand Tavano Bob Grossman	Ferrari 250 GT California

RIVALRY AND REVENGE

1960–1969

As the 1960s dawned one team dominated Sportscars, Formula 1 and Le Mans – Ferrari. The Italian team run by Enzo Ferrari had previously won the Le Mans 24 hours in 1949, 1954 and 1958 before being defeated by Aston Martin the following year. In 1960 the team returned in full force and dominated the 1960, '61, '62 and '63 races. At the same time in America, Henry Ford II was rebuilding the Ford brand. Ford were doing this by entering the world of motorsport. They began to compete in NASCAR, and Ford engines were being used in Indy car, but Henry Ford II wanted more. He looked to Europe. In late 1963, Enzo Ferrari went bankrupt and had no other choice but to sell to another company. Henry Ford II jumped at the chance and wanted to buy. At first, the relationship between Enzo and the Ford executives was respectful and friendly, and with not much time left it looked like the deal would go ahead and Ford would buy Ferrari. The company would be known as "Ford-Ferrari" and Enzo would have control over the race team. But the deal fell apart, because Ford wanted final say on which races to enter. Ferrari pulled out of the deal and sold to Fiat instead, upping the price from $10 million to $18 million. Ford were left feeling bitter about this and Henry Ford II said, "We are going to race and beat him whatever the cost." Gradually it became clear that Ford were going to build the fastest car in the world to beat Ferrari at Le Mans.

After this, Ford teamed up with British engineer John Wyer to create a car to beat Ferrari. The result was a car called the GT40 – 40 because its overall height was 40 inches – and it was a modified Lola Mk6 with a 4.7 litre engine. The driver line-up for the 1964 race was world class. In the #10 Ford was young New Zealand Formula 1 driver Bruce McLaren, joining him was three time Le Mans winner and Formula 1 world champion Phil Hill. The #12 car was driven by Richard Attwood and Jo Schlesser. Despite the Ford challenge, John Surtees took pole with a new lap record in his Ferrari. To make matters worse for the Ford team, Phil Hill stalled off the line and was now 70 seconds back. Problems continued with the Hill/McLaren Ford, the issue being a blocked carburettor. Once this was fixed, the pair battled their way back up to sixth place behind the Ferraris and the leading Porsche. But the Porsche dropped back with clutch problems, leaving the Ferraris in the lead. By the early morning, Phil Hill's Ford had gearbox problems putting him out of the race. So once again Ferrari took a dominant and relatively unchallenged 1–2–3 victory. In fourth place was the GT class winner, Dan Gurney and Bob Bondurant in the Shelby Daytona Cobra Coupe. After the Le Mans failure, Henry Ford II took the project away from John Wyer and gave it to the Shelby America team. Carroll Shelby, the 1959 Le Mans winner, had stopped racing in 1960 and founded the Shelby America race team, Mr Ford believed Shelby was the perfect choice for a team manager. By 1965, the GT40 had been heavily modified, most notably now using 427 cubic inch 7-litre V8 engine and was ready to take on Ferrari at Le Mans.

1965 was the first year the Shelby American Ford GTs took on Ferrari. John Surtees had been on the pace in practice behind the wheel of his new Ferrari 330 P2, but Phil Hill took pole in his 7-litre Ford. America had live coverage of the race for the first time in 1965. The two Shelby American Fords were setting a blistering pace at the front – Bruce McLaren setting lap record after lap record. But the success was short lived, as the Fords proved unreliable. As night fell, Ferrari took the lead, but they too started to develop problems and by the morning the factory Ferraris were out of the race. The lead was held by North American Racing in a Ferrari 250LM who took a shock victory, with private Ferraris locking out the top three places.

Pos	No	Team	Drivers	Chassis
1	21	North American Racing Team	Masten Gregory Jochen Rindt Ed Hugus	Ferrari 250 LM
2	26	P. Dumay	Pierre Dumay Gustave Gosselin	Ferrari 250 LM
3	24	Ecurie Francorchamps	Willy Mairesse Jean Blaton	Ferrari 275 GTB

In 1966 Ford meant business! They had won the Daytona 24 hours and the Sebring 12 hours earlier in the year with a world class driver line-up. For Le Mans, team Shelby America will lead the ford program with three GT40s. NASCAR team Holman Moody will run three other GT40s, as well as two entries from Alan Mann racing. Ferrari had prepared seven prototypes entered by various teams, but all were prepared at the Ferrari factory. There were two new factory-entered 330 P3 cars and one privately run 330 P3 from Luigi Chinetti. Chinetti and three other private teams had also entered a 365 P2. But the main two cars to challenge the Fords were the factory backed 330 P3s.

At four o'clock on the 18th of June in 1966, Henry Ford II waved the official start flag, and the race was underway. As the cars screeched away from the line and completed the first lap, Ken Miles had to pit after a slow first lap. When Miles got in the car he banged his head and broke the door catch so the door would not close. He re-joined after it was fixed. Graham Hill took the lead but after lap three the Shelby American Ford of Dan Gurney retook the lead. The best Ferrari was currently in fourth. The cars pushed hard, Gurney and Miles battled for the lap record as Miles was making a recovery. An hour and a half into the race Bruce McLaren pitted with a tyre problem. He was contracted to race on Firestone tyres while the other Fords were on Goodyears. Bruce made the call and switched to Goodyears and set off on a hot pursuit of the leaders. Soon into the evening, Miles had shattered the lap record taking 7 seconds off the previous years' time. Going into the night Ken Miles and Denny Hulme took the lead as the Ferraris chased. Le Mans is notorious for the challenging night hours. Six hours into the race the Ferraris were leading 1–2 after the pitstops, but heavy rain came and many cars crashed. The pace slowed, but Ken Miles didn't and began to take time out of the Ferraris. Before long he was back in the lead in his #1 Ford. To make matters worse for Ferrari, they soon began to suffer with overheating. At halfway it was Ford 1–2–3–4. Miles/Hulme lead ahead of, Gurney/Grant, then McLaren/Amon, and Bucknum/Hutcherson. This set things up going into the morning.

As day dawned at Le Mans all the front running Ferraris were out of the race after a gruelling and tough night. The Ford drivers were all given an instruction – no inter-team racing. The only thing that could change the finishing order would be a mechanical problem. But, at 4:10 am, the leading Ford driven by Ken Miles had to pit with a brake problem. He drove so fast and aggressively that he had to have a brake change. The team worked over the car with precision, changing the front disc brakes and re-joined the race in the lead. Then at 7:30 am, the team changed the back brakes too. By this time Miles was down to second place behind Gurney and Grant. But a few minutes after 9 am, Gurney pitted with a radiator leak. He was out. This put Miles and Hulme back in the lead with McLaren and Amon in second. Well down in third place was the Holman Moody Ford driven by Ronnie Bucknum and Dick Hutcherson. It became clear that Ford was going to win and the plan now was to reduce the speed and finish the race. Ford were victorious and they had beaten the might of Ferrari. Bruce McLaren and Chris Amon were declared the winners ahead of Ken Miles and Denny Hulme.

Pos	No	Team	Drivers	Chassis
1	2	Shelby American	Bruce McLaren Chris Amon	Ford GT40 Mk.II
2	1	Shelby American	Ken Miles Denny Hulme	Ford GT40 Mk.II
3	5	Holman & Moody	Ronnie Bucknum Dick Hutcherson	Ford GT40 Mk.II
4	30	Porsche System Engineering	Jo Siffert Colin Davis	Porsche 906/6 LH
5	31	Porsche System Engineering	Hans Herrmann Herbert Linge	Porsche 906/6 LH

After Ferrari's Le Mans defeat in 1966, the team regrouped and came back in full force. At the first round of the 1967 season, the Daytona 24 hours, Ferrari dominated, finishing 1–2–3. 1966 Le Mans winner, Chris Amon left Ford to join Ferrari in sports cars and Formula 1. Team Shelby America entered two new GT40 MKIV, the #1 car driven by Dan Gurney and Le Mans rookie A.J. Foyt. Foyt had just won the Indianapolis 500 for the third time two weeks earlier. Mark Donohue and 1966 winner Bruce McLaren drove the #2 Ford. Various other GT40s were entered by privateers. Ferrari arrived with three new 330 P4 cars as well as seven other older models entered by private teams. Mario Andretti qualified fastest, leading a Ford 1–2–3–4–5 ahead of John Surtees in a Lola. Ronnie Bucknum was first away after an efficient Le Mans start in his #57 Ford. The Chaparrals were running well, so too were the Ferraris in the initial stages. After the first round of pitstops, A.J. Foyt had the lead in the #1 Ford. As night began to fall on Le Mans, Amon's

Ferrari suffered a puncture. During the night, after Andretti took a pitstop, he came racing out of the pit lane and spun at the Dunlop curve hitting three sandbanks. He broke three ribs. Another Ford hit the side of Andretti's abandoned Ford and Bruce McLaren picked up a puncture after running over debris. In the early morning, Phil Hill's Chaparral developed an oil leak dropping him out of winning contention. By 10 am only sixteen cars were still in the race, Gurney and Foyt were comfortably in the lead. The pair held on to win by four laps and secured the first all American victory at Le Mans. The Ferrari of Ludovico Scarfiotti and Mike Parkes came home second ahead of the Belgian entered Ferrari. Bruce McLaren and Mark Donohue were fourth ahead of four Porsches.

The 1968 race was delayed from June to September due to protests and civil unrest in France. This was also the first race since 1964 not to feature a factory Ford. However, JW Automotive had entered various GT40s as well as other private teams. But the Porsche 908 of Jo Siffert took pole and lead the opening laps, ahead of three more Porsches. As night began to fall on Le Mans, two Gulf Racing Fords were steadily gaining places and moved into the lead. At halfway the #9 Ford had comfortable four lap lead ahead of the Matra team. But early in the morning, the Matra team had a puncture and the third place Alfa Romeo had suspension failure. This promoted the Swiss Porsche team to second place. The JW Automotive Ford GT40 took a comfortable five lap win ahead of the two Porsches. This was a third straight win for Ford at Le Mans.

Pos	No	Team	Drivers	Chassis
1	9	JW Automotive Engineering	Pedro Rodriguez Lucien Bianchi	Ford GT40
2	66	Squadra Tartaruga	Hans-Heinrich Steinemann Dieter Spoerry	Porsche 907LH
3	33	Porsche System Engineering	Rolf Stommelen Jochen Neerpasch	Porsche 908LH

Since its first Le Mans in 1964, the GT40 had aged significantly against the competition, and some thought it was outdated. In 1969 new prototypes from Porsche, Ferrari and Matra were threatening its Le Mans crown. This was also reflected in qualifying, as Porsche took the top three grid positions, the best GT40 was down in thirteenth place in the hands of Jacky Ickx. Ickx was convinced that the traditional Le Mans start was outdated and dangerous so, he did not run across the track at the start like the other drivers. Instead, he walked and took his time to fasten his seatbelt. He was the last to get away. Meanwhile, on the first lap, John Woolfe crashed and died because he had not done up his seatbelt properly. The fuel from his car leaked in front of Chris Amon's Ferrari, which caught fire. Luckily he was unhurt but forced to retire. Up the front it was five Porsches leading with a Lola placing sixth. Through the night the Ickx/Oliver Ford was steadily gaining places and by 10:15 am, they were in the lead. But the Herman/Larousse Porsche was making time. Both the Ford and Porsche teams put their best drivers in the cars for their last stints. With one hour to go it was game on for the win. The Ford of Ickx was in the lead with twenty-four laps estimated until the 24 hours was up. But the fuel capacity of the Ford was only twenty-three laps. Ickx had to drive economically and fend off the challenge from Hans Herman. The pair swapped places multiple times but Ickx held on to lead. Jacky Ickx and Jackie Oliver won by a just a few seconds, only 120 metres. But the death of John Woolfe overshadowed the race and raised the safety concern over Le Mans and motorsport.

Pos	No	Team	Drivers	Chassis
1	6	JW Automotive Engineering	Jacky Ickx Jackie Oliver	Ford GT40
2	64	Porsche System Engineering	Hans Herrmann Gérard Larrousse	Porsche 908LH Coupé
3	7	JW Automotive Engineering	David Hobbs Mike Hailwood	Ford GT40
4	33	Equipe Matra – Elf	Jean-Pierre Beltoise Piers Courage	Matra-Simca MS650
5	32	Equipe Matra – Elf	Jean Guichet Nino Vaccarella	Matra-Simca MS630

The 1970 race started with the #20 and #25 917 Porsches in the lead. But after one lap the #25 takes the lead. From then on the rain came and many crashed. The Ferrari's struggled and

Porsche dominated from then on. But the rain stayed through the night. As day breaks only half the started cars are still going. The #23 car took the lead and kept it till the end. 1970 was a landmark first win for Porsche, having come so close to victory in 1969. Hans Herman and Richard Attwood made history on Sunday 14th June.

GROUP 5 AND GROUP 6

1970–1979

After Ickx's protest in 1969, the race officials abolished the traditional Le Mans start. For 1970 drivers started in their cars with the engines off, the following year a rolling start system was introduced. After Porsche took their first Le Mans win in 1970, there was no stopping them in 1971 with Gijs van Lennep and Helmut Marko winning in the 917K. Porsche were also dominating the WSCC taking the title in 1969, '70 and '71. The late sixties and early seventies saw multiple changes to the track. The first major change since 1932 came in 1968, when a new chicane was added at the end of the lap. This slowed down the cars considerably across the start/finish straight, meaning the pit crews were safer. In 1971 a pit wall was installed splitting up the three-lane racetrack – it was now two lanes with a pit road. In 1972 a twisty section was added at the end of the lap, which we now know as the Porsche Curves. Defending champions Porsche retired their 917K and replaced it with a series of upgraded 908 and 908/02 models. Matra stepped up their endurance programme with a new and bold driver line-up including Formula 1 world champion Graham Hill to partner Frenchman Henri Pescarolo. The French team entered four cars and were favourites to win having decided not to enter the opening eight races of the WSCC to focus on preparation for Le Mans. This worked because in qualifying they took the first three places on the grid. Pescarolo took the lead from second place on the grid at the start and opened up a commanding lead. Things were not perfect though for Matra as in the early stages the #12 was forced to retire with engine failure. A miscalculation in the evening for the #16 meant the car ran out of fuel and needed to be pushed to the pits. The team did manage to get going again but later retired with transmission failure in the last hour. However, there was no stopping Pescarolo and Hill who took a dominant eleven lap victory from the #14 car. Third place went to the Siffert ATE Racing Porsche. Matra became the first French car to win Le Mans since 1950. However, the race was overshadowed by the tragic death of Swedish racer Jo Bonnier who died behind the wheel of his Lola T280. After Matra's success they decided to compete in more of the WSCC races in 1973. But at Le Mans there was more competition for the French team as Ferrari decided to enter their 312 P with 1969 winner Jacky Ickx leading the line-up. Ickx and Brian Redman had won the previous round at the Nurburgring and the battle was set at Le Mans. But the Matra team remained the champions, of Le Mans with Henri Pescarolo teaming up with Gérard Larrousse to take victory. Ferrari finished second with their least preferred car after Ickx and Redman's car had engine issues in the final hour. Matra topped off the success with the world sports car title later in the year. The following year, 1974, the Matra team and Henri Pescarolo were still the team to beat in sports car racing. Once again Pescarolo and Larrousse took victory six laps ahead of the Martini Racing 911 Porsche. Having taken the WSCC title in 1973 and '74, Matra decided not to run an endurance programme and focus on providing engines in Formula 1.

The 1975 race was in jeopardy of even starting due to the American fuel-crisis hitting Europe in a bad way (the 1974 Daytona 500 was shortened and was known as the Daytona 450). To address this issue, the ACO announced new regulations for the race including a rule that all cars needed to go at least twenty laps before refuelling. As an indication, in 1974 the winner stopped every sixteen laps for fuel. Because of this the race is often referred to as the "Le Mans economy run." Jacky Ickx and Derek Bell took pole in their Gulf racing Mirage. Bell mastered the rolling start but could not fend off the other Mirage driven by Vern Schuppan. However, Bell could maintain a consistent pace of under 4 minutes. Therefore, after the first round of pitstops, Ickx, having taken over from Bell, took the lead. The battle though was still on as by the fourth hour the two Mirage cars were separated by just 2 seconds. During the night and early morning, the #11 Mirage of Ickx and Bell had built up a sizeable lead but during the morning the car started to develop vibration issues. By 2:30 pm the problem was so bad they had to make an unscheduled pitstop. The team franticly repaired the exhaust system and the second placed Ligier closed in. Also, the electronics were playing up in the #10 Mirage and it looked like the race might slip away. However, both the British cars managed to complete a few slow laps to finish the race first and third. Only a lap separated the winning car of Ickx and Bell and the second place Ligier.

The 1976 race set the tone of what was to come for Le Mans in the next few years, a battle between Porsche and Renault-Alpine. Like in Formula 1 the Renault team were the first to dominate with turbo power and although it didn't finish the race, the French team did have an intense battle for the lead with Porsche at the start of race. This was also the first race Jean Rondeau entered and raced his own cars coming third in class. The Martini Porsche team won with Jacky Ickx and Gijs van Lennep at the wheel with a victory of a whopping eleven laps to the 1975 winning team, Mirage.

The 1977 race is one of the most legendary in Le Mans history. It is most remembered for Jacky Ickx's tremendous night shift to get back into winning contention, but there was more to the 45th Le Mans 24 hours than that. Heading into the race, Renault were the clear favourites, having entered four cars over two teams after months of preparation just for Le Mans. Winning on home soil would be a huge deal for the French team to win. They had world class drivers including former Le Mans winner Derek Bell, Formula 1 drivers Jacques Laffite and Patrick Tambay. Jacky Ickx led the Porsche charge with Henri Pescarolo in their 936. Porsche entered two 936 cars as well as several upgraded 935s entered by various private teams. Local driver and team owner Jean Rondeau entered a team of his own Inaltera cars sponsored by a local wall paper company for the second year. There was also significant interest from Chevron, Mirage, and Lola. However, as expected Renault locked out the front row with a record-breaking pole lap from Jean-Pierre Jabouille in the #9 with a time of 3:31.7. The Porsche of Ickx and Pescarolo started third ahead of two more Renaults. But, from lap one of the race it did not go to plan for the French team. Halfway through the first lap, the #16 car caught fire after an oil-line split. Ickx had made a move on the first lap, positioning his Porsche into second place past a Renault. But the Porsches were fragile and after just sixteen laps the Barth/Haywood car came into the pits with a faulty fuel pump. The car dropped to forty-first place while it was being repaired. A few hours later, Henri Pescarolo, having taken over from Ickx, was battling for the lead with Jabouille. But Henri over-revved the engine of his 936 which broke a conrod and the Porsche was forced to retire. The Porsche team decided to move Ickx from the #3 car to the #4 car driven by Barth/Haywood. Meanwhile, Renault held the 1–2–3 positions.

Ickx, Barth and Haywood were fifteen laps back on the leaders heading into the night. Porsche told Jacky Ickx to go for it since there was nothing to lose. Over the next 13 hours, Ickx drove at an incredible pace, gaining on the leaders at nearly 10 seconds a lap. By midnight, he was fifth, six laps behind the leaders. The best placed Mirage was three laps behind them. Renault were still favourites for victory, but at 3 am things started unravelling. Tambay's engine gave up due to lack of oil pressure, but at the halfway mark things still looked good for Renault and a home victory. Ickx was still on the move, now he was up to third. As dawn broke a heavy shower caught out most drivers, including the race leader. Jabouille spun at the Ford chicane but luckily for him stopped before hitting anything. By ten past nine, Ickx had finished his sprint-marathon having driven the maximum allowable time for one driver. Minutes later the leader Jabouille came into the pits with a smoking engine. He was out. Things got even worse for Renault as at 12 pm the inherited leader stopped in the pits for longer than expected. The #4 Porsche gained a few laps and was now only two laps behind. Then all of a sudden, the Renault gave up. Porsche now had a comfortable 16 lap lead over the Mirage team and looked set for an amazing comeback victory. But as if things could not get any more dramatic, the leader came into the pits with less than an hour to go. The number #4 Porsche, now with Barth at the wheel, lost five laps as the mechanics tried to sort out the problem. With ten minutes to go the car left the pits and completed one agonisingly slow lap. The regulations said that every car must cross the line to be classified as finishing. Barth completed two careful laps to coast over the line and take an incredible comeback victory. Mirage was next ahead of a 935 Porsche and Jean Rondeau's Inaltéra LM77.

Pos	No	Team	Drivers	Chassis
1	4	Martini Racing Porsche System	Jürgen Barth Hurley Haywood Jacky Ickx	Porsche 936-77

Pos	No	Team	Drivers	Chassis
2	10	Grand Touring Cars	Vern Schuppan Jean-Pierre Jarier	Mirage M8
3	40	JMS Racing ASA Cachia	Claude Ballot-Léna Peter Gregg	Porsche 935
4	88	Inaltéra	Jean Rondeau Jean Ragnotti	Inaltéra LM77
5	5	A. de Cadenet	Alain de Cadenet Chris Craft	De Cadenet-Lola LM77

In 1978 Porsche and Renault-Alpine returned with four cars each, but this time it was the German cars that proved to be unreliable and the Renault team asserted dominance from the beginning. Jacky Ickx once again had early problems with his Porsche and so was moved to the other Porsche driven by Bob Wollek and Jürgen Barth. The team managed to climb the order but second place was the best they could do in their 936-78 Porsche. This time the French Renault-Alpine car was not denied of victory with Didier Pironi and Jean-Pierre Jaussaud at the wheel. Porsche came second and third with the #4 Renault coming fourth. The big news heading into the 1979 race was that movie legend Paul Newman would be competing for Dick Barbour Racing in a Porsche 935. Early in the race the Mirage team took the lead but the 935 Porsches looked competitive. During the night a huge storm came and lots of cars crashed out. During the night Jacky Ickx was well placed until a drivebelt broke and he had to have outside assistance from the Mulsanne marshals. Therefore he was disqualified. Newman was running in second place but with 20 minutes to go the car developed a bad misfire. Rolf Stommelen at the wheel managed to come to a stop in front of the finish line and waited for the leading Kremer Racing car to cross the line. This meant he didn't have to risk doing another lap, the race being won by Klaus Ludwig, Don Whittington and Bill Whittington

PORSCHE DOMINANCE

1980–1989

When the 1980s began we still had the Group 5 and Group 6 regulations continuing on from the 1970s. Le Mans was round seven of the 1980 WSCC and Porsche were dominating, however heading into Le Mans there was strong competition from Frenchman Jean Rondeau. He had entered his own cars at Le Mans since 1976 and won the GTP class in 1977 and '78. Rondeau had designed a prototype for a six-wheel race car but for the 1980 race he decided on a more conventional design, his team came close to winning Le Mans in 1979 but a range of technical problems put his cars out of the race. Heading into the 1980 race, Jean Rondeau was aiming to become the first person to win Le Mans in a car he had designed, built and raced in a team which he owned. His chances increased when the Mirage team had decided not to enter Le Mans meaning his toughest competition would be one of the Porsches, all were private entrants as the factory teams had pulled out. Joest Racing entered a Porsche 908/80 driven by the experienced pair of Jacky Ickx and Reinhold Joest. The race started with very wet conditions. The racing was difficult in the early stages and the rain never really stopped throughout the 24 hours. The race lead went back and forth in the early stages, but the Ickx Porsche seemed to have the upper hand. During the night the two Rondeau cars started to close in on the leading Porsche and the race was on. The #16 Rondeau took the lead and was helped when the Porsche had an issue. Ickx in the Porsche tried to make up for lost time but in the end Jean Rondeau and Jean-Pierre Jaussaud took victory by two laps ahead of the Ickx/Joest Porsche. The #17 Rondeau finished third and the small French team made Le Mans history. Then in 1981 Porsche did return to the top step of the Le Mans podium with Jacky Ickx and Derek Bell winning in the 935/82. This was the last year before the change to Group C regulations.

The fiftieth Le Mans 24 hours was all about the legendary 956 Porsche. The German team arrived as clear favourites and Rondeau, although having the lead in the early hours, couldn't fend them off. The race proved to be a perfect one for Porsche they took a clean sweep with Jacky Ickx and Derek Bell winning the overall podium, and the GT classes were won by privately entered Porsches. This was also the first race the legendary 956 "Rothmans" Porsche won at Le Mans and the seventh overall victory for the constructor.

Pos	No	Team	Drivers	Chassis
1	1	Porsche System	Jacky Ickx Derek Bell	Porsche 956
2	2	Porsche System	Jochen Mass Vern Schuppan	Porsche 956
3	3	Porsche System	Jürgen Barth Hurley Haywood Al Holbert	Porsche 956

After the 1982 triumph, it was clear that the Porsche 956 was the car to beat in sports car racing. The Group C category suited the German team and a battle emerged between the factory teams and the privately entered teams. The 1983 race was the fourth round of the World Championship and the Porsche 956 had won the previous three rounds. Jacky Ickx and Derek Bell were aiming for their third straight Le Mans win and fourth as a pair. There was a close battle between the #3 and #1 Rothmans Porsches. With only a couple of hours to go Derek Bell had managed to unlap himself from the leading #3 car. The win looked possible for Bell and Ickx, especially when the leader had an overheating issue. However, Vern Schuppan, Hurley Haywood and Al Holbert managed to hold on by less than a lap from Ickx/Bell. The Porsche 956 locked out the top eight positions at Le Mans and won every round of the 1983 WSCC season. There was controversy heading into the 1984 race when the Rothmans Porsche team boycotted the ACO over fuel regulations and pulled out of the race in protest. This left Joest Racing to take victory and they made it back-to-back victories in 1985 with the exact same car. Rothmans Porsche were back on the top step for 1986 and this was the first win for the 962C car. Porsche once again won the WSCC. Heading into the 1987 race Jaguar were seen as winning contenders as well as the Sauber Mercedes team. Jaguar had won the first four races of the '87 season but Le Mans didn't work out for the British team. Porsche once again won the race, but Jaguar dominated the championship winning eight of the ten races.

There was a real chance that Jaguar could win the 1988 race for the first time since 1957 with their new XJR-9. Sauber Mercedes looked like strong contenders for the race having won the first round of the 1988 WSCC. But before the race began Mercedes pulled out of Le Mans because of tyre blowouts from their Michelins. This left a straight fight between the TWR Jaguars and Porsche AG who were starting in the top three positions on the grid with the 962C. The Porsches made a good start but on the first lap Jan Lammers in the #2 Jaguar made up positions to take second place. The battle was on and the race would be a big duel between the two manufacturers. Soon he would move into the lead with the top three cars being covered by less than a second in the opening stint. After a dodgy first pitstop from Porsche, the #2 Jaguar built up a lead. Not too much would change during the night, however both Porsche and Jaguar lost one of their cars with reliability issues. Joest Racing moved up into third place during the mid-morning, but the victory fight was very much between two cars; the Jaguar #2 and Porsche #17. The Jaguar team had gearbox issues and the #3 car had dropped out of the race. So, Jan Lammers in the leading #2 Jaguar made a crucial decision with 40 minutes to go that he was not going to change gear. This saved the race for the British team. The other two Jaguars formed up with the leader but not for the traditional photo finish. Instead, they were there to help push the #2 over the line if there was a problem. Thankfully there was not, Jan Lammers, Johnny Dumfries and Andy Wallace won with the #17 Porsche just 170 metres behind. This was one of the closest finishes at Le Mans.

The 57th edition of the 24 hours of Le Mans, held on 10–11 June 1989, was a fierce battle between Jaguar, Porsche, Mercedes and Nissan. The Jaguars led early on, but an oil leak gave the lead to the #9 Porsche, which would be kept until the 10th hour. Jaguar regained the lead until a gearbox change put them out of the top three. It resulted in 1–2 finish for Sauber-Mercedes. The #63 C9 driven by Jochen Mass, Manuel Reuter and Stanley Dickens took the chequered flag for the win.

Pos	No	Team	Drivers	Chassis
1	63	Team Sauber Mercedes	Jochen Mass Manuel Reuter Stanley Dickens	Sauber C9
2	61	Team Sauber Mercedes	Mauro Baldi Kenny Acheson Gianfranco Brancatelli	Sauber C9
3	9	Joest Racing	Hans-Joachim Stuck Bob Wollek	Porsche 962C

INNOVATIONS

Le Mans is famous for testing new designs and pushing boundaries of technology. Here are some ground-breaking innovations which are now found on road cars everywhere. These new technologies used on racing cars have led to safer and better road cars as well as an advantage in a race.

1926 – FOG LAMPS

It is not unusual for a part of the circuit to be shrouded in mist as dawn breaks. To overcome this problem, The engineers at Lorraine-Dietrich added a third lamp in the centre of the grille and because of the advantage gained by having better visibility, the car went on to take victory.

1929 – ROAD MARKINGS

In 1929 white lines were painted on the middle of the road to help the drivers. At the time, white lines were not used on the surrounding roads. This was another first for Le Mans.

1949 – SEATBELTS

In 1949 seatbelts were first used at Le Mans. This was an experiment, but the decision came after a series of serious accidents pre-war. The safety benefits of this became clear and today every road and race car made by law must have a seatbelt.

1952 – DIRECT INJECTION ENGINE

In 1952, Mercedes introduced a system – originally developed by Bosch for aircraft – that was capable of improving the efficiency of petrol engines. Petrol was injected directly into the combustion chamber, avoiding fuel losses and optimising combustion. The famous 300 SL was equipped with this technology when it won in 1952 with Hermann Lang and Fritz Riess behind the wheel.

1953 – DISC BRAKES

Jaguar were expected to win the 1952 race, but after the Mercedes dominated, Jaguar were left behind. So, they developed brake discs, replacing drum brakes and with superior stopping power, took the type C to victory.

1967 – SLICK TYRES

Michelin brought a major innovation to the racing world when it invented "slicks" – tyres with a smooth tread, providing greater traction on a dry track.

1970 – ROTARY ENGINE

The technology was introduced in 1970 on a Chevron-Mazda, powered by a 200 bhp, 983 cc twin-rotor engine which failed after just 4 hours of the race. In 1991, however, the design came good when the rotary-engine Mazda 787B drove to victory.

2006 – DIESEL

Since it was invented in the late 19th century, the diesel engine has always been associated with commercial vehicles. However technical developments such as direct fuel injection, and turbos have boosted performance and cut fuel consumption. Audi used this to full advantage and won the race in 2006 with a diesel-powered car called the Audi R10 TDI.

2013 – HYBRID

Audi took victory in 2013 with a hybrid engine – part electric, part petrol working together. This meant the Audi could go a greater distance between fuel stops and go faster. The #2 Audi R18 e-tron quattro driven by Allan McNish, Tom Kristensen and Loïc Duval won with the #3 car third. No car since has won the 24 hours without a hybrid engine.

GROUP C AND LMGT1

1990–1999

The 1990s marked a new era of sports car racing, with the first big change coming on the Mulsanne Straight at Le Mans as two new chicanes were added to reduce top speed. This came in the new set of rules from the Fédération Internationale du Sport Automobile (FISA) stating that no straight should be longer than 1.2 miles. The race was also withdrawn from the WSCC and because of this defending champions Sauber Mercedes decided not to enter the 1990 race. In qualifying Japanese team Nissan were on the pace taking pole and dominated with four cars in the top five. Porsche was still seen as strong contenders as well as Jaguar. Toyota were not seen as in winning contention, but still strong opposition for the leading manufacturers. Despite the dominance in qualifying, the Nissan team suffered problems very early in the race. The #25 car, which had qualified fifth, had a gearbox issue on the way to the grid and was not able to complete the first lap of the race. Despite this problem Nissan dominated the early stages of the race with the Jaguars moving forward. Nissan struggled with reliability and all their cars suffered a number of issues throughout the night. In the night the #3 Jaguar took the lead and after the #1 suffered with engine trouble, Martin Brundle was transferred from that car to the #3. This idea was to maximise the chances of their leading car and this worked – Jaguar claimed their seventh Le Mans win with John Nielsen, Price Cobb and Martin Brundle at the wheel. The #16 Repsol Brun Motorsport Porsche was ready to claim second place, but with 15 minutes left of the race, the engine gave up and Jaguar claimed a 1–2 result. Third place went to a privately entered Porsche driven by an all-British crew of David Sears, Tiff Needell and Anthony Reid. Only one Nissan finished the race placing fifth with Toyota sixth.

Peugeot led at the start, but it did not last long as the #6 came into the pits with fuel pressure problems. Then the #5 Peugeot had a broken engine. Both the Peugeot's are out. After 4 hours the Mercedes were running 1–2–3. Jaguar held fourth spot. But their victory hopes were severely damaged during the night. Fuel consumption issues meant they had to hold back to stay in the regulations. As day broke Mercedes were in the lead, but that did not last long because at midday the #1 car had over heating issues. Then at 12:54 an alternator breaks on the lead car and they are out. Johnny Herbert put in a triple stint in his Mazda to make sure of victory. Mazda did win and became the first Asian team to win Le Mans. Herbert would miss out on the podium due to exhaustion and dehydration.

Pos	No	Team	Drivers	Chassis
1	55	Mazdaspeed Co. Ltd.	Volker Weidler Johnny Herbert Bertrand Gachot	Mazda 787B
2	35	Silk Cut Jaguar	Davy Jones Raul Boesel Michel Ferté	Jaguar XJR-12
3	34	Silk Cut Jaguar	Bob Wollek Teo Fabi Kenny Acheson	Jaguar XJR-12

In the early stages of the race the 1991 Le Mans winning Mazda team dominated the opposition taking the lead. But Le Mans is a marathon not a sprint and it was the #1 Peugeot came back into the picture and it was leading by night fall. The crew of Mark Blundell, Derek Warwick and Yannick Dalmas looked set for victory but with 7 hours left the #1 car had an ignition problem and two pitstops were required to sort it out. But they held on to beat Toyota to take victory. The French crowd saw Peugeot come first and third at France. 1992 was the last full year of the WSCC and Peugeot dominated winning all but one race. The FIA made the tough decision to cancel the WSCC due to the lack of entries because of the tight regulations. The regulations for a new series in 1993 were rushed through and the ACO created the "Le Mans Prototype" category. Group C cars were still allowed to take part as well as a GT category. Peugeot were still the team to beat entering three 905 EVOs. The only other team in the new "C1" category were Toyota who had brought four TS010 cars. The new GT category worked well and a total of twenty-seven cars entered the race from a range of top-class manufacturers including Porsche 911s, Jaguar XJ220s and Venturi 500 LMs. This was a big improvement from the year before where only thirty cars started the race, now in 1993 a total of forty-eight cars started. The race was a battle between the Peugeot and Toyota, who were aiming to win their first Le Mans. The Toyotas looked strong and with the earlier problems for Peugeot, heading into the night Toyota had the advantage. However the French cars were catching and by the morning they held an impressive 1–2–3 position. Meanwhile Porsche were leading in the GT class, and the Larbre Compétition team won. Back at the front in the C1 category Toyota pushed Peugeot hard but the French cars locked out the podium with Éric Hélary, Christophe Bouchut and Geoff Brabham taking victory.

Moving on to 1994, the old WSCC was well and truly in the past and to keep sports car racing alive a new set of regulations was needed. The ACO expanded the GT car class and decided to make it the top category known as LMGT1. 1990 Group C cars were still allowed in principle design, however they now had to be open top and have a completely flat underside. This would now be known as LM-WSC. Porsche was one of the first to commit to the LMGT1 and they used their engines in the Dauer 962 LM. The regulations stated that road going versions were to be made and the Dauer 962 was the first. The 1994 race was a jumble because there was no championship, so the structure of the race was not clear. The race proved to be a battle between LMGT1 Dauer 962 Le Mans cars and the LMP1/C90 Toyota 94C-V. After the 1991 win for Mazda, there had been significant interest from Japan with Toyota and Nissan focusing on endurance racing, but it would not be win 1994 for either constructor as Porsche took another Le Mans win with Yannick Dalmas, Hurley Haywood and Mauro Baldi at the wheel.

The regulations became more clear heading into 1995 and McLaren entered their new super car into the GT1 category.

The car was called the F1, not to be confused with Formula 1, and the roadgoing version had three seats in the front with the driver sat in the middle. This was an unconventional approach to a super car layout, but it was designed by the legendary Gordon Murray and the road car produced 630 bhp with a top speed of 240 mph. The GTR version, which would compete at Le Mans in 1995, was designed to be reliable with seven being made to compete for the race. The race itself was incredibly wet, one of the wettest in Le Mans history. The main battle was between the GT cars and the prototypes, with the two Welter Racing run WR LM94 cars leading the way with their Peugeot engines. In the early stages the Courage Compétition Porsche was giving chase to the two leading WR LM94s. The best McLaren started ninth and the GT cars were a lot slower than the prototypes in the early stages of the race, but the fuel regulations for the GT cars would benefit them throughout the race. The rain came in the second hour, and this favoured the GT cars. The first twist of the race came when the Welter Racing cars had two separate incidents meaning both of were out. Mario Andretti was at the wheel of the #13 Courage but unfortunately, he spun and the team dropped down the order. This was an unusual mistake from the racing legend, but he was able to continue after an unscheduled pitstop. After that the McLarens had a 1–2–3 lead heading into the night, and the battle raged on all morning and with an hour to go Andretti had caught up to third. But with 30 minutes to go Derek Bell's #51 McLaren had to pit from second overall with a transmission issue. McLaren were not denied victory as the British team took their first Le Mans win with Yannick Dalmas, Masanori Sekiya and JJ Lehto the drivers ahead of the Courage team with the #51 McLaren third. After the defeat for the Prototype cars, Joest racing won overall victory racing in 1996 the following year with the TWR Porsche WSC-95 car. The same chassis car won the following year in 1997 and this, notably, was the first time Tom Kristensen won the 24 hours and it was his debut Le Mans. The 1998 race was looking to be one of the most competitive to date with the LMGT1 and LMP1 regulations being updated so that both categories were fairly similar, and both could have an equal chance of victory. Mercedes, Porsche and Toyota would all battle in the GT1 class while BMW would aim for LMP1 honours battling against the Ferrari 333 SP. Qualifying was close but the GT1 cars seemed to have the edge and Mercedes were on pole ahead of Toyota and two Porsche 911 GT1-98 cars. However, at the start of the race everything was jumbled with the LMP1 BMWs making progress in the background and the Mercedes losing the lead to

Toyota. Nissan were also in the LMGT1 category and began to make progress towards the front of the field. The Toyotas pushed hard in the early stages leaving Mercedes behind. The German team were focused on setting a good lap time in qualifying, that their car was still partly set up for qualifying and the aerodynamic system in the car didn't work so well with a full fuel load. During the night the 911 GT1-98 Porsches were reliable and managed to stay out of trouble which is so critical for a good race at Le Mans. The competition was faster than Porsche, but all the Mercedes, BMW and Toyota cars retired with mechanical problems. This left the Ferrari 333 SP to win the LMP1 class and finish eighth overall with Wayne Taylor, Eric van de Poele and Fermín Velez the drivers. In the GT1 category – and overall – Porsche was unstoppable and lead most of the morning taking a dominant 1-2 result. Third, fifth and sixth went to Nissan with their R390 GT1. Porsche left sports car racing at the end of the year and didn't return to prototype racing until 2014.

Pos	No	Team	Drivers	Chassis
1	26	Porsche AG	Laurent Aïello Allan McNish Stéphane Ortelli	Porsche 911 GT1-98
2	25	Porsche AG	Jörg Müller Uwe Alzen Bob Wollek	Porsche 911 GT1-98
3	32	Nissan Motorsport	Aguri Suzuki Kazuyoshi Hoshino Masahiko Kageyama	Nissan R390 GT1
4	40	Gulf Team Davidoff McLaren	Steve O'Rourke Tim Sugden Bill Auberlen	McLaren F1 GTR
5	30	Nissan Motorsport	John Nielsen Michael Krumm Franck Lagorce	Nissan R390 GT1

The 1999 race was one of the most action-packed in Le Mans history, with drama starting before qualifying when in free practice Mark Webber in his Mercedes flipped up into the air. Amazingly the car was rebuilt and ready to go to race. The battle was still going to be intense with Mercedes, Toyota, BMW, Nissan and Audi all taking part. Toyota took pole and were determined to take their first Le Mans victory after years of trying and battled hard with the Mercedes in the early stages. The BMW kept close and the race was shaping up to be one of the best in years, but as the Toyota and Mercedes were battling for the lead, disaster struck. Peter Dumbreck's Mercedes flipped up into the air the same way a Mark Webber's had and landed in the nearby trees at Mulsanne, thankfully the Scottish driver was OK. Heading into the night the race looked like it was Toyotas to lose and at midnight the #2 car had a collision with a backmarker putting them out of second place. BMW still had the lead and were under pressure from the #3 Toyota, but a puncture in the final hour put the Japanese car out of winning contention. So, after a hectic 24 hours the #15 BMW driven by Joachim Winkelhock, Pierluigi Martini, and Yannick Dalmas took victory. The race was the last of the LMGT1 era as LMP became the main focus for the new millennium.

THE SCIENCE

WHY DID THE MERCEDES FLIP IN 1999?

In 1999 Mercedes entered the 24 hours of Le Mans in their new CLR prototype. They had problems immediately. In Thursday qualifying, Formula 1 driver Mark Webber was driving when the car took off and flew into the air. The car landed back on the track and Webber walked away from the accident. Mercedes made some adjustments to the suspension and added aerodynamic fins to the front. It made no difference because in practice the same thing happened to Webber again and in the race Peter Dumbreck in the #5 shot into the air and flipped three times before landing in some nearby trees. Incredibly Mark and Peter were both fine after their crashes.

EXPLANATION

Drag is a force that slows a moving object down, the less drag the more performance can be gained from the engine. But by reducing drag, the downforce can be compromised. In 1999 Mercedes wanted no drag, so for the CLR the wheelbase was shortened creating a bigger overhang at the front and back. This made the car unstable, and the car would rock back and forth. On all three occasions when the car flipped, Mark and Peter had been in the slipstream of another car. This disrupted the downforce, causing the car to lean back and eventually flip. After Peter Dumbreck's crash 5 hours into the race, the German team pulled out the remaining cars from the race and have not entered since.

DOWNFORCE

Downforce is air resistance pressing on a car increasing pressure on the tyres to benefit cornering grip. Downforce is important to a Le Mans car, especially in the fast sections like the Porsche curves or the Esses.

SLIPSTREAM

Slipstream, known as drafting in the USA, is when a car travels close behind another to benefit from thinner air. When the lead car travels, it punches a hole in the air. The car traveling close behind can gain extra speed from the thin air left behind by the lead car.

SLICK TYRE

Modern slick racing tyres are two to three times wider than road car tyres and are smooth with no tread. Rapid acceleration and deceleration means the tyre heats up quickly, and becomes hot and sticky, so they grip well enough without the need for tread.

NISSAN GTR LM NISMO

The Nissan GTR LM Nismo did not hit the headlines with results, however it was one of the most interesting cars to race at Le Mans. Nissan had always been experimental at Le Mans, often occupying garage 56 used for experimental car designs. But in 2015, Nissan launched the GTR LM Nismo to compete in the LMP 1 class. The car only took part in one race, the 2015 Le Mans, but it was definitely an eye-opener. The most radical thing about this car is that the power is driven to the front wheel drive. The front splitter helps channel the air down a tunnel through the car. The whole side of the car is one big cross section which helps reduce drag, as well as a slippery shape on the top of the car. The hybrid system is mechanical – completely different to the other LMP 1 cars. It is a flywheel that spins at 52,000 RPM, which is kept in a vacuum because the fly-wheel tips would travel well over the speed of sound. This comes with its own traction control system. Nissan have the option to send the hybrid power to the front wheels or the rear. Due to the engine being in the front, the shortest exhaust system was to have it come out before the windscreen. This helps optimise wind flow going down the car.

An unusual front engine, front wheel drive design gives the car a 65:35 weight ratio. This creates efficient downforce at the front of the car.

LMP1

2000–2009

At the dawn of the new millennium Audi returned in full force after their success of a Le Mans podium in 1999. For the 2000 race they entered three R8 prototypes, that locked out the overall podium with Frank Biela, Emanuele Pirro and Tom Kristensen the winners. At this stage Audi were the only big manufacturer in Le Mans and also dominated the 2000 American Le Mans series championship. Panoz Motor Sports were close competition to the German team and going into 2001 there was significant interest from Chrysler, MG and Bentley. Bentley were making a racing comeback having not competed at Le Mans since 1933 and two cars called the Speed 8 were entered. However, the efficient Audi team were able to win again with the same trio of drivers as the year before. The #2 car came second with the best Bentley placing third and winning its class. The MG and Panoz cars suffered problems putting them out of the race in the early stages. Frank Biela, Tom Kristensen, and Emanuele Pirro were on top form and managed to win the race again in 2002 in the dominant R8 Audi. The 3.6 Turbo V8 was one of the most efficient engines on the grid and the car was really setting a high standard for sports cars in the years to come. 2002 was marked the first time in Le Mans history that the same driver line-up had won three years in a row. Bentley once again finished the race and claimed fourth overall behind the Audis. Fifth and sixth places went to the Dallara SP1 cars run by the Oreca team. The 2002 race was another turning point in Le Mans history because the track layout had changed significantly. After the Dunlop Bridge, the circuit turned to form a sweeping sequence of corners which would join onto the Esses. After the race the Bentley team worked hard and came back fighting for the 2003 event taking pole and second place on the grid. The race also featured an experimental car which was run on 100% bioethanol fuel. The Bentleys maintained the lead from the start of the race being pushed hard in the early stages by the Dome from Racing team Holland. The Bentley team were able to maintain a good pace throughout the race and could take the fight to the dominant Audis. The toughest competition for the Bentley cars were the private Audi team of Champion Racing, because the factory Audi Sport team had decided not to enter this season. But they were no match to the two Bentleys, and the #7 car won ahead of the #8 car. Champion racing came third and the Ferrari team won in the GT category. This was Bentleys first overall Le Mans victory since 1930. The Bentley team celebrated their Le Mans victory the same way they did back in 1927, by bringing the winning car into the Savoy hotel dining room to have dinner with it!

Heading into the 2004 race, Audi were once again favourites for the victory and this year their main competition came from the private team Pescarolo Sport. Bentley were not back to defend their Le Mans crown, but Kristensen was and back in an Audi. The Pescarolo team, founded and operated by four-time Le Mans winner Henri Pescarolo, were not on the pace of the Audi team and the German cars came first, second and third with Kristensen claiming his fifth consecutive Le Mans win and sixth in total – a new record. However, the record didn't last long because the following year he was back on the top step with his co drivers JJ Lehto and Marco Werner in their Audi R8 LM. This would be the last Le Mans triumph for the R8 as they decided to enter the 2006 with a new car, the R10 TDI. As soon as the

2005 race was over, the Audi team switched focus to the new car with a radical new design of a diesel engine.

WRC champion Sebastien Loeb is racing in Pescarolo Sport. But the #7 Audi took pole. At the start the two Audis led followed by the Pescarolo's. Soon after Audi started to dominate. As evening fell on Le Mans the #7 Audi got pushed into the garage with a small engine issue but it would continue. Night at Le Mans and the #16 Pescarolo had its electrics checked as the #8 Audi leads. The #7 car recovered to third as day broke. In the morning the #8 Audi got stopped at the end of pit road because it did not have a working light, Audi fixed this with a new front. At five o'clock in the afternoon the #8 Audi took victory, Emanuele Pirro, Frank Biela and Marco Werner.

Pos	No	Team	Drivers	Chassis
1	8	Audi Sport Team Joest	Frank Biela Marco Werner Emanuele Pirro	Audi R10 TDI
2	17	Pescarolo Sport	Sébastien Loeb Éric Hélary Franck Montagny	Pescarolo C60 Hybrid
3	7	Audi Sport Team Joest	Rinaldo Capello Tom Kristensen Allan McNish	Audi R10 TDI

For 2007 it was all change with Peugeot making a sports car comeback with the 908 HDi FAP and they meant business taking pole with their #8 car ahead of the #2 Audi. This year Pescarolo raced another 908 Peugeot and had a chance of rivalling the factory teams. The race started dramatically when Sébastien Bourdais went off at the first corner and handed the lead to the #2 Audi. The battle was fierce and at one point during the first hour all the Audis lead but the Peugeots had good pace. The Audis had superior traction and the Peugeots started to slip back during the night. They suffered from some unlucky mechanical failures and collisions on track. But it was not easy for the Audi team either and with 7 hours left the leading Audi driven by Rinaldo Capello lost a rear wheel and was out of the race. This put the #1 Audi in the lead driven by Frank Biela, Emanuele Pirro and Marco Werner who won the race ten laps ahead of the #8 Peugeot. The Pescarolo team came third, a fantastic result for them having stayed out of trouble. The Peugeots pace was good and the Audi team knew that they were a serious threat with the French cars sleek design, the Audi R10 was seen as slightly outdated. Audi returned the following year to defend their Le Mans crown entering a total of three cars across their two teams (one based in Europe and one based in America). The Peugeot team were confident in their design and after a build-up year in 2007, a Le Mans victory looked very possible in 2008. On average the French cars were 3 seconds a lap quicker than the Audis and it looked an impossible task for the German team to claim a fifth consecutive victory. But the Peugeots were not the most reliable and after 12 hours, two of the three cars had been delayed with various problems. But the #7 car was in the lead and on a charge and it was looking likely that the distance record could be broken.

In second place was the #2 Audi with three Le Mans veterans at the wheel: Allan McNish, Rinaldo Capello and Tom Kristensen. The Audis pushed on hoping for trouble at the front. They were in luck because in the morning it started to rain. Kristensen was at the wheel and began to charge, leaving nothing on the line and pushing as hard as his car could go. The Peugeots struggled in these conditions and this only motivated the #2 team. During the pitstops the Audi took the lead and with only a few hours left to go the track started to dry up. Peugeot took a gamble and went onto slick tyres, but the track was still too damp leaving the Audi team to take an unlikely victory with the #7 Peugeot still on the lead lap. This was one of the closest Le Mans finishes in history and after coming so close to success, Peugeot knew they could win in 2009. Confident in their engineering, they entered the same 908 HDi FAP the following year. Audi however entered the new R15 TDI and another exciting race was waiting to happen. But new fuel rules favoured Peugeot and they used that to full advantage to dominate qualifying and maintained a pace which the Audis could not keep up with. Despite the #7 having a puncture early in the race, the Peugeot team had no more dramas and managed to take a magnificent 1–2 result ahead of the #1 Audi a distant third. Audi were defeated and Peugeot took their first Le Mans win since 1993.

Pos	No	Team	Drivers	Chassis
1	9	Peugeot Sport Total	David Brabham Marc Gené Alexander Wurz	Peugeot 908 HDi FAP
2	8	Team Peugeot Total	Franck Montagny Sébastien Bourdais Stéphane Sarrazin	Peugeot 908 HDi FAP
3	1	Audi Sport Team Joest	Tom Kristensen Allan McNish Rinaldo Capello	Audi R15 TDI
4	007	AMR Eastern Europe	Jan Charouz Tomáš Enge Stefan Mücke	Lola-Aston Martin B09/60
5	11	Team Oreca Matmut AIM	Olivier Panis Nicolas Lapierre Soheil Ayari	Oreca 01

LE MANS ON THE SILVER SCREEN

LE MANS

Year: 1971

Starring: Steve McQueen

Director: Lee H. Katzin

Running time: 106 Minutes

Arguably the most iconic Steve McQueen film, *Le Mans* captures the speed, the passion and the excitement of the race. McQueen stars as an American racing driver called Michael Delany and drives for the Porsche team in this fictional 24 hours of Le Mans race. The movie was filmed at the Circuit de la Sarthe between June and November in 1970 and lots of the footage is from the 1970 race. McQueen was a huge fan of cars and motorsport, having wanted to make a movie about grand prix racing called *Day of the Champion* but after the release of *Grand Prix*, the idea was abandoned. McQueen was a keen racer himself and had considered turning professional after doing a British Touring Car Championship race in a BMC Mini finishing third. He regularly competed in offroad motorcycle racing when he was not filming for a movie. His passion for vehicles worked its way into most of his movies, most notably *The Great Escape* when he jumped a fence on a motorcycle. McQueen insisted on doing all his own stunts in movies including the *Bullitt* car chase. He attended the 1969 24 hours of Le Mans as a spectator and got his first taste of driving sports cars a year later when he raced, and finished second, in a Porsche 908 at the Sebring 12 hours. McQueen went back to Le Mans and started work on the *Le Mans* movie a year later. During the 1970 race, the car McQueen finished second at Sebring in was specially adapted to carry cameras so action onboard shots from the race could be used in the film. The Porsche 908 was entered by Solar Productions and managed to finish the race as well as collecting lots of footage for the film. Over the next five months filming began properly with stunt drivers and revolutionary filming techniques used to create the finished product. During most of the filming, there was no clear script and tempers were fraying because McQueen had a vision of a film about racing and racing cars, whereas Cinema Center Films wanted a clear story with racing as the setting. McQueen eventually made the film the way he wanted, the racing sequences were the main feature and the film became an all-time classic.

LE MANS 66

Year: 2019

Starring: Matt Damon and Christian Bale

Director: James Mangold

Running time: 152 Minutes

Le Mans 66, also known as *Ford V Ferrari* in some territories, was a 2019 film starring Matt Damon and Christian Bale made by 20th Century Fox. The film was based on the 1960s rivalry of Ford and Ferrari at Le Mans with the climax being the 1966 Le Mans 24 hours. Matt Damon played racing driver and automotive designer Carroll Shelby while Christian Bale starred alongside as legendary racing driver Ken Miles. The film shows the friendship of the two as well as the desire to beat the Ferrari racing team. The film was originally going to star Tom Cruise and Brad Pitt before the project fell apart due to the budget being deemed too high. But the idea was too good to be abandoned and James Mangold was given the role of director. The film was inspired by the book *Go Like Hell* written by A.J. Baime and some of the movie was filmed at Le Mans as well as the majority of the film being shot in California. The movie features action packed racing scenes as well as lots of replica Le Mans cars and together with an excellent soundtrack captures the spirit of 1960s racing.

TRUTH IN 24

Year: 2008

Starring: Allan McNish, Rinaldo Capello and Tom Kristensen

Director: Keith Cossrow and Bennett Viseltear

Narrator: Jason Statham

Running time: 98 Minutes

Truth in 24 was a documentary movie about Audi sport and their preparation for the 2008 Le Mans 24 hours. The film focuses on the two races before Le Mans (Sebring and Monza), preparation and the 2008 Le Mans 24 hours. The film builds up the tension between Peugeot and Audi in the thrilling race. Action film actor Jason Statham narrates the movie and several members of the Audi team were interviewed for the film. Truth in 24 was premiered before the 2009 race.

TRUTH IN 24 II

Year: 2012

Director: Rob Gehring

Narrator: Jason Statham

Running time: 83 Minutes

Truth in 24 II was a sequel documentary made by Audi sport focussing on the 2011 Le Mans 24 hours. The race that year was another exciting battle with the Peugeot team for the overall victory and the movie shows it every step of the way from the perspective of the Audi team. The film was launched in 2012 and Jason Statham returned to narrate it.

LE MANS 3D

Year: 2016

Starring: Mark Webber, André Lotterer, Darren Turner and Benoît Tréluyer

Director: James Erskine

Running time: 90 Minutes

Le Mans 3D is a documentary movie focussing on the 2015 Le Mans 24 hours featuring behind the scenes access of the race. German Audi driver André Lotterer is defending champion and three time Le Mans winner but this year the challenge is even bigger than before. Leading the Porsche team, hoping to take the fight to Lotterer, is former Formula 1 race winner Mark Webber. Webber raced at Le Mans in 1998 and 1999 but failed to finish on both occasions, this year he wants to put that right and take victory. Can Audi keep their Le Mans crown, or can Porsche win their seventeenth Le Mans 24 hours?

MICHEL VAILLANT

Year: 2003

Starring: Sagamore Stévenin, Peter Youngblood Hills and Diane Kruger

Director: Louis-Pascal Couvelaire

Running time: 103 Minutes

Michel Vaillant is a series of French car racing comic books created in 1957. In 2003 a French film was released starring Sagamore Stévenin as a racing driver called Michel Vaillant and the film featured scenes that were shot at the 2002 Le Mans 24 hours. The film is action packed with rivalries, rallying, circuit racing scenes leading to a race at Le Mans. Unfortunately, the film was not seen as honouring the comics it was based on, however the film was praised for the photography in the racing scenes.

PAUL NEWMAN

Paul Newman was a very successful American actor who won an Academy Award, three Golden Globes and one Emmy Award. In 1968 he starred as a racing driver at the Indy 500 in the movie *Winning*. This is where he first fell in love with motorsport and first professionally entered a race in 1972. He then raced in the SCCA national championship for the majority of the 1970s having lots of success before racing at Le Mans in 1979. He drove with Rolf Stommelen and Dick Barbour in a Porsche 935 finishing second overall and first in class. After this Newman won his class at the 1995 Daytona 24 hours before he co-founded Newman/Haas Racing with Carl Haas.

PATRICK DEMPSEY

Hollywood actor Patrick Dempsey has raced at Le Mans four times with his best result being second in the GTE AM class in a Porsche at the 2012 race. He also won the 2015 6 hours of Fuji WEC race and now runs Dempsey Proton Porsche. During the 2022 Le Mans race he said "The learning curve is very steep, it is just so competitive here and the whole overall experience is so intense. The celebrities, the movie stars Paul Newman and Steve McQueen really brought a lot of attention to Le Mans, but it is no joke, when you get here it is serious business."

JACKIE CHAN

Jackie Chan is a Chinese actor who co owns Jackie Chan DC Racing with Asian Le Mans champion David Cheng. The cars were run at Le Mans by Jota Sport from 2017 to 2020, with a Le Mans class victory coming in 2017.

JOURNEY TO LE MANS

Year: 2014

Starring: Simon Dolan, Oliver Turvey, Harry Tincknell, Allan McNish, Mark Webber and Sam Hignett

Director: Charlotte Fantelli

Narrator: Sir Patrick Stewart and Tiff Needell

Running time: 96 Minutes

Journey to Le Mans is a documentary made by Fantelli Productions about Jota Sport and their dramatic 2014 season. The film stars British businessman Simon Dolan who is passionate about Le Mans and races for the Jota Sport team. The film follows the underdog British team through the challenges of achieving success in sports cars with an insight to how the team is run. Legendary English actor Sir Patrick Stewart narrates the movie with Tiff Needell as well as commentary from Radio Le Mans being used throughout the race. The movie ends with Jota securing their first-class victory at Le Mans in 2014 with Simon Dolan, Oliver Turvey and Harry Tincknell at the wheel. The film was directed by award winning director Charlotte Fantelli who went on to direct another Le Mans movie in 2018 called *Gentleman Driver.*

JOTA SPORT

Jota Sport is a British Sports Car team founded in 2000 by Sam Hignett and John Stack. In 2004 the team raced at Le Mans, but an accident in the 22nd hour put them out of the race. After mixed results in 2005, '06, '07 and '08 the team stepped back from Le Mans until 2011. Jota Sport raced at Le Mans in an Aston Martin that year but the team changed direction in 2012 by entering the LMP2 class with their famous Zytek. They finished the race for the first time in 2013, seventh in class and finished the ELMS season third. Heading into the 2014 season they were seen as title contenders and a class victory at Le Mans was their aim. The driver line-up for the ELMS season was a mix of youth and experience, with Simon Dolan returning for his sixth season with Jota Sport, determined to take a Le Mans class victory, Filipe Albuquerque and Harry Tincknell joined the team with Marc Gene scheduled to drive at Le Mans instead of Albuquerque. The season started really well with Tincknell taking pole position at the first round in Silverstone and the race was under control until a collision with a backmarker sent Dolan into the wall. It was a very heavy impact, but Dolan escaped with minor injuries. The car on the other hand needed a full rebuild before the race at Spa in one week later. Their race was mighty, and the team finished second in class. Imola was the next race on Jota Sports 2014 schedule and after a midrace strategy change, Dolan, Tincknell and Albuquerque took their first win of the season. Le Mans was the next race, but things got off to a bad start with a tyre blowout in testing the week before, but the car was ready for qualifying. But at the last minute, Gene was not able to race for Jota as he was needed to race for the Audi LMP1 team after Loïc Duval had a massive accident and was unable to race. 2013 Jota driver and McLaren F1 test driver Oliver Turvey was called upon at the last minute to take the place of Gene, meaning Jota were able to compete. Tincknell qualified second in class and took the lead in the early stages of the race before a downpour of rain and a technical problem put them down to thirteenth in class. But the team were not out of the race and through the night they started to gain places and by the morning were in contention for a podium finish. After a clever fuel strategy by the Jota team, Turvey was leading the class with less than one hour to go, and they held on to take an emotional LMP2 class victory in 2014. In 2015, the team finished second in class at Le Mans and won the ELMS championship in 2016 with G-Drive racing. For 2017, '18 and '19 Jota partnered with Jackie Chan DC Racing and had huge success in WEC and won their class at Le Mans in 2017. 2020 and 2021 saw two more LMP2 podiums but 2022 was the most convincing victory at Le Mans yet. Formula E champion Antonio Felix da Costa qualified third in class and on the grid said, "I have 24 hours to pass two cars." After a strong start he was up to second in class and he inherited the lead after a superb pitstop by the Jota team. After the first hour da Costa stretched the lead to nearly 3 minutes before handing over to Will Stevens 3 hours into the race. Da Costa, Stevens and Roberto González pushed very hard, and along with the whole Jota crew didn't make a mistake for the rest of the race. The #38 car lead all but the first fifteen laps in class over the whole 24 hours. They took victory by nearly a minute and a half, it was one of the most dominant wins in Le Mans history. Meanwhile, the #28 Jota car started thirteenth in class and during the night worked their way up and finished the race third, making it an impressive double podium for the team.

2022 Le Mans

2015 Le Mans

THE HYBRID ERA

2010–2020

The hybrid era of Le Mans rivals the 60s and Group C as the best of all time. Audi were determined to fight back from their defeat by Peugeot in 2009 and entered a new car. It was based on the R15 TDI but this time Audi had chosen to focus on aerodynamic efficiency and the fuel tank cooling system. These upgrades meant the German manufacturer could be able to take the fight to the Peugeots who had not made such big changes as Audi heading into the race and were relying on their past success. Sébastien Bourdais in the #3 Peugeot took pole and lead from the start but Audi pushed hard. During the afternoon there were suspension problems for the #3 Peugeot which put it out of the race but Peugeot still held first, second and third place. Going into the evening, the #7 Audi had a spin involving a backmarker. As night fell on Le Mans, the #1 Peugeot had a long pitstop to fix the cars starter. Then it had a spin and went into the gravel. As dawn broke, the #2 Peugeot stopped on the Mulsanne Straight on fire! The #9 Audi pushed on and got the lead which they kept till the end. Mike Rockenfeller, Timo Bernhard, and Romain Dumas took victory setting a new all-time distance record. In the 24 hours they went 397 laps covering a distance of 3361.618 miles and an average speed of 140mph.

2011 was another significant year at Le Mans because it was the first race since 1992 to be part of a championship season. The 2011 race was third round of the Intercontinental Le Mans Cup and although we did not know this at the time, it would be the last time with Peugeot racing in LMP1. Audi returned with a brand-new car – a closed cockpit R18 TDI Ultra. The car debuted earlier on in the season at Spa Francorchamps and took pole, but in the race, it could only manage third as Peugeot took the top positions. Audi took pole at Le Mans and right from the beginning two Audi's lead the race with Peugeot close behind. Peugeot had good fuel efficiency and could do one lap more per stint than the Audis. Fifty minutes into the race Alan McNish had a terrible accident, the #3 Audi collided with a back-marking Ferrari and flew into the air. It was a miracle that the car did not go over the other side of the tyre wall. More bad luck for Audi came during the night Mike Rockenfeller had a crash on the Mulsanne straight. During the morning all three Peugeot have a pitstop at the same time. The #2 Audi takes the lead, and the #9 Peugeot is the closest contender to challenge the Audi. Entering a new phase of the race, Peugeots #7 and #8 try to slow the #2 car down. They block the Audi on the straights and in the corners. Dangerous driving showed Peugeot were desperate, but at the finish the #2 Audi of Marcel Fässler, André Lotterer and Benoît Tréluyer took victory by 13.854 seconds (700 metres). 2012 was the eightieth running of the race and the third round of the 2012 FIA World Endurance Championship (WEC), with thirty of the race's fifty-six entrants contesting the championship. The LMP1 battle did not feature Peugeot but instead Toyota aiming to take the challenge to the Audi team. Also, various privateer teams entered the LMP1 class including Strakka, Rebellion, Pescarolo and Oak. It was Audi who locked out the front row ahead of the Toyota and they successfully lead the opening stages of the race, but Toyota showed promising pace. After a series of small setbacks for Audi, by the fifth hour Lapierre in the Toyota was battling for the lead with Tréluyer in the #1 Audi. Heading into the evening, Anthony Davidson in the #8 Toyota made contact with a Ferrari sending the prototype into the air, it flipped over in the air and landed back on the ground, the right way up, before smashing straight into the tyre wall. Davidson was taken to hospital, and he was found was to have a fractured vertebra. There was a 70-minute safety car period to clear up the Toyota and once racing did get underway there was another incident. The leading Audi and Toyota were battling before Nakajima's #7 Toyota collided with the DeltaWing and was sent into the barrier. The Toyota was forced to pit for repairs and lost three positions while the DeltaWing was forced to retire. After this it was a relatively straightforward run to victory for last year's winning trio in the #1 ahead of the #2 and #4 Audis.

The 2013 race was overshadowed by the tragedy of Danish driver Allan Simonsen who died just 10 minutes into the race in his Aston Martin. The race was the 90th anniversary of Le Mans and once again was a battle between Toyota and Audi for the overall glory. As evening fell, the #3 Audi had a spin, and lost a back tyre. Then the night came at Le Mans and 7 hours in, the #2 Audi took the lead but Toyota push hard. As day breaks the track is damp, but the #2 Audi still leads. There was still hope for Toyota, but the #7 Toyota went off into the gravel. Loïc Duval, Tom Kristensen, and Allan McNish take victory. Tom Kristensen won his ninth 24 hours of Le Mans in the 90th anniversary of the first race.

2014 was one of the best Le Mans in the modern era, throughout all the classes. Audi and Toyota returned in the LMP1 category and re-entering for the 2014 WEC season were Porsche with a new prototype car called the 919 Hybrid as well as continuing in the GTE PRO category. Rebellion Racing once again returned to the LMP1 category with their non-hybrid R-One and would be battling with Lotus for the best independent team result. Both teams made up the LMP1-L category for teams without a hybrid system. Audi were defending champions of the WEC but the first two rounds of the 2014 season had not gone their way. Toyota were leading the standings but Porsche looked strong and the hybrid system of the 919 was promised to be competitive at Le Mans. Things got worse for Audi in free practice when Loïc Duval crashed and flipped above the barriers destroying the car. Duval was injured and unable to race but the car was rebuilt and Marc Gené was moved from the Jota Sport LMP2 team to race for Audi. Oliver Turvey was brought in to replace Gené at Jota. The qualifying result was Toyota–Porsche–Toyota–Porsche with Audi fifth, sixth and seventh on the grid. The start of the race was sunny and dry with a crowd of 245,000 expecting a three-way manufacturer battle for victory. At the start André Lotterer made quick progress and moved into podium position before the rain came. A huge storm swept the track in the evening and an accident happened on the Mulsanne Straight with the #3 Audi and #8 Toyota. The Toyota was able to continue but the Audi retired on the spot. The rain cleared and by nightfall the #7 Toyota had a minute lead over the two remaining Audis. But the Japanese car lost drive 10 hours into the race and was forced to retire. The two Audis and two Porsches battled for the rest of the race until the leading #20 Porsche stopped with a broken anti-roll bar and retired. This left André Lotterer, Marcel Fässler and Benoît Tréluyer to take victory in their #2 Audi ahead of the #1. In the LMP2 category Jota Sport showed their class to take their first Le Mans victory. In the GTE PRO category, Ferrari held on to take victory ahead of Corvette. Before the 2015 Le Mans, Nissan announced they would be making a comeback to sports car racing in the LMP1 category with their new GTR LM Nismo. The car was unconventional compared to the other prototypes and they were not seen to be in winning contention. The battle for the win was between the three automotive giants: Porsche, Audi and Toyota. The Audi team came back fighting for title and the #7 car driven by Benoît Tréluyer, Marcel Fässler and André Lotterer won the opening two rounds at Silverstone and Spa. But in qualifying for Le Mans the Porsche team were on form claiming the top three positions on the grid. The Audi team were fourth, fifth and sixth on the grid with the WEC champions Toyota next. The non-hybrid cars from Rebellion and ByKolles were next ahead of the two Nissans. The Nissan team were making their WEC debut, and they were over 20 seconds behind pole position. Unfortunately, things didn't get any better for them and none of the cars finished. The race was an intense battle between Audi and Porsche with the Toyota team struggling for overall pace. The Porsche team managed to outpace the Audi team to claim the first and second positions. Nico Hülkenberg, Nick Tandy and Earl Bamber took victory in the 919 Porsche, their first win since 1998. Audi came third and fourth with the Toyotas a few laps back. This was a real turning point in the World Championship as Porsche went on to have an incredible run of form and won all the remaining five races and take the title. Audi came second in the World Championship with Toyota third. Nissan didn't race their GT-R LM again after the Le Mans disappointment.

Porsche 919 locked out the front row, but with 5 minutes before the start rain came down and the first 52 minutes were behind the safety car, when racing got underway the #6 Toyota took the lead and soon after this the #7 Audi lost 20 minutes in the pit garage due to turbo issues. As night fell on Le Mans the #6 Toyota and the#1 Porsche had a huge battle for the lead. But then the Porsche 919 had to come into the pits with water pump issues. In the morning the #5 Toyota passes the #2 Porsche to take the lead and keeps it until 5 minutes left in the race. Starting the last lap, heartbreakingly for the Toyota team, the car loses power on the start/finish straight. The #2 Porsche soars past and takes the lead with one lap left. Le Mans has chosen its winner and it is Porsche! Marc Lieb, Romain Dumas and Neel Jani took victory and Porsche claimed their 18th overall win at Le Mans.

Pos	No	Team	Drivers	Chassis
1	2	Porsche Team	Marc Lieb Romain Dumas Neel Jani	Porsche 919 Hybrid
2	6	Toyota Gazoo Racing	Stéphane Sarrazin Mike Conway Kamui Kobayashi	Toyota TS050 Hybrid
3	8	Audi Sport Team Joest	Loïc Duval Lucas di Grassi Oliver Jarvis	Audi R18

Audi pulled out of the championship after the 2016 season meaning the battle for the title, and Le Mans victory, came down to a Porsche verses Toyota. The weather was incredibly hot and all the LMP1 cars suffered from technical problems during the race. The heat took its toll and after three and a half hours into the race, the #2 Porsche had to spend 65 minutes in the pit garage to fix a front axle. This put them well down the order. The Toyotas lead but, in the night, all three of the Japanese cars were forced to retire with various mechanical problems. So, by the morning the #1 Porsche driven by Andre Lotterer was leading the race until he stopped with an engine issue on the Mulsanne straight and was forced to retire. So, with 5 hours left of the race the Jota Sport car in the LMP2 class took the overall lead of the race. This was the first time an LMP2 car had led at Le Mans but by the afternoon the #2 Porsche overtook Ho-Pin Tung in the #38 Jota to win by just one lap. The Jota sport crew came first and second in class and in GTE PRO Aston Martin beat Corvette in a dash to the line to win. The Corvette had suffered a puncture on the last lap and slipped behind #67 Ford GT. This Le Mans will be remembered as one of the most unexpected races in Le

Mans history with nearly all the LMP1 cars self-destructing. After the 2017 Le Mans Porsche announced they would leave the LMP1 category at the end of the season. This left Toyota as the only hybrid cars in the entire race in 2018 and they looked set to take their first Le Mans victory. The regulations were changed slightly heading into the race to help the non-hybrid cars of the Rebellion, SMP, DragonSpeed and ByKolles teams. The big news at the beginning of the season was the two-time F1 champion Fernando Alonso would be joining the Toyota team. At the start of the race Lotterer tried to get in front of the Toyotas in his Rebellion but was forced off. From that point on the Toyota cars were dominant and they took a 1–2 result with Alonso at the wheel of the winning car. The following year was almost identical with the two Toyotas heading off into the distance and claiming a perfect result. The 2020 race was held in September for the first time since 1969, this was because of the global pandemic. With Alonso gone from the Toyota team at the end of the 2019 season, Brendon Hartley joined the #8 team with Sébastien Buemi and Kazuki Nakajima. They took victory but this season they had significant opposition from Rebellion Racing, who managed to split the two Toyotas and finish second with the #7 Toyota in third. However, these Toyota victories were seen by some as hollow because they were the only team with hybrid power, meaning no other car could realistically challenge for the victory. After the 2020 season a new set of regulations called Hypercar were announced.

KEN MILES

THE BEST DRIVER NEVER TO WIN LE MANS?

Ken Miles was a sports car engineer and driver with incredible talent. Born in 1918 in England, he raced motorbikes before he drove tanks in the Second World War. After the war he moved to Los Angeles in 1952 and won the 1953 SCCA championship in an MG he designed and built. Miles was a key member of the Shelby Cobra race team in the early 60s – because he was a great engineer and driver. When Carroll Shelby was handed the Le Mans Ford project, he knew Miles would be perfect to engineer the new car. Within weeks Miles and the rest of Shelby America had made significant improvements to the GT40, but Miles felt the car was not ready for Le Mans. However, in 1965 he raced with Bruce McLaren at Le Mans, but gearbox trouble put him out of the race. The next year, he won the 24 hours of Daytona, and the 12 hours of Sebring in the Ford GT Mk. II. Several months later, sharing the drive with Denny Hulme, Miles was leading the 1966 24 hours of Le Mans, but Ford executive Leo Beebe, wanted a photo of three of their cars crossing the finish line together. Miles was ordered to slow down. This angered him, however he did play the "team game" and let second place Bruce McLaren catch up as well as the third place Ford. Ken Miles in the blue Ford and Bruce McLaren in the black Ford crossed the finish line at the same time creating the picture the Ford Motor Company wanted. But the "photo-finish" meant Miles and Hulme lost because the #2 Ford had covered a bigger distance having started further back on the grid. Le Mans is after all a distance race. Miles felt crushed and would never come so close to win Le Mans again. Tragically, the following August he died, testing the Ford J-car at Riverside Raceway.

OTHER GREAT NON-WINNERS

STIRLING MOSS

Le Mans starts: 10

Best result: 2nd (1953, '56)-

Sir Stirling Moss is seen as the greatest driver never to win the Formula 1 world championship, despite coming close. Moss made his Le Mans debut in 1951 and came close to winning when driving for Jaguar in 1953. However, a fuel problem put him back at the start. In 1955 Moss and Juan Manuel Fangio were dominating the race, but after the tragedy, Mercedes pulled out from the race. Moss missed out on his best chance at victory. A second place and class win the following year was his best result when driving in an Aston Martin DB3S. 1959 Moss showed how much of a team player he was when he opted to be the hare and drive a flat-out race knowing his Aston Martin would break down. This was to outpace the Ferraris and allow his Aston Martin team mates to take victory.

MARIO ANDRETTI

Le Mans starts: 8

Best result: 2nd (1995)

Mario Andretti is one of motorsports most iconic, famous and successful drivers of all time and about the only success missing from his racing career is a Le Mans victory. Andretti had his best chance to take victory on his second visit driving the Ford MKIV but a rare error in the night took him and two more Fords out of the race. Indy 500 champion Andretti had better luck in the 80s at Le Mans with Porsche. He finished third in 1983 and sixth in 1988 but his best result came in 1995 driving a Courage C34. He spun in the early stages of the race but drove magnificently through the night with his co-drivers Bob Wollek and Éric Hélary to finish second overall and first in class.

BOB WOLLEK

Le Mans starts: 30

Best result: 2nd (1978, '95, '96, '98)

Bob Wollek is one of the most unlucky drivers at Le Mans. The French driver made the switch from skiing, having won three gold medals, and entered Le Mans thirty times but never had the luck needed to win. "Brilliant Bob" spent most of his sports career with Porsche as well as some drives for Toyota, Courage, Jaguar and Lancia. Wollek did taste some success at Le Mans, taking four class victories and six overall podiums however, the overall victory slipped away on so many occasions. Wollek won a total of seventy-six races in his motorsport career and should be seen as a racing hero.

ANTHONY DAVIDSON

Le Mans starts: 13

Best result: 2nd (2013)

Anthony Davidson started the Le Mans 24 hours no less than thirteen times, but bad luck meant an overall win slipped away on so many occasions. Davidson managed to score two overall podiums and a class podium with the LMP1 Toyota team, which he was part of for six years, and one LMP2 class podium with Jota Sport. He has had success in sports car racing and managed to take the WEC LMP1 title in 2014 having taken four wins in the season. Anthony Davidson is still part of a great sports car team, this time in the commentary box with Martin Haven and Graham Goodwin.

JOHN SURTEES

Le Mans starts: 4

Best result: 3rd (1964)

John Surtees first started racing on motorcycles and was very successful, winning a total of seven motorcycle world championships. After this he decided to race in Formula 1 and was quickly asked by Enzo Ferrari to race for his team. In 1964, his second year with Ferrari and fifth year of Grand Prix racing, he took the title becoming the only man to win world championships on two and four wheels, but Le Mans was the race which got away from him. Surtees was the fastest driver, but reliability issues stopped him from winning. In late 1965 Surtees had a terrible accident at Mosport in Canada but came back with Ferrari for the 1966 season. However, the team doubted his ability, and he walked away from the Italian team two days before Le Mans in 1966. He went on to race for Honda in Formula 1 and won the 1967 Italian Grand Prix.

VIC ELFORD

Le Mans starts: 8

Best result: 6th (1973)

Vic Elford was one of the fastest drivers in his era and a totally fearless driver, especially on the demanding Nürburgring circuit. He came close to winning Le Mans on a number of occasions too, especially in 1969 when he and co-driver Richard Attwood led most of the race before retiring with 4 hours to go. Elford pushed hard in the opening stages the following year and took the lead at the start in the Porsche 917 longtail. But bad luck struck again with an engine problem with 6 hours to go. There were other occasions where Elford came close, but an overall victory just slipped away from the great driver.

DRIVERS WITH THE MOST WINS OF ALL TIME

TOM KRISTENSEN

Le Mans starts: 17

Le Mans wins: 9

Teams raced for:
- Audi Sport Team Joest
- Audi Sport North America
- ADT Champion Racing
- Audi Sport Japan Team Goh
- Team Bentley
- Team BMW Motorsport
- Joest Racing

One of the greatest drivers in sports cars, touring cars, and Formula cars, Tom Kristensen won at Le Mans on his very first appearance. Kristensen was racing Formula 3000 in 1997 when a late call meant he had a chance to race a Porsche for Joest Racing at Le Mans. He drove a tremendous stint during the night and scored a sensational victory with his teammates Michele Alboreto and Stefan Johansson. "Mr Le Mans" then won six 24 hours in a row, with works Audi R8s in 2000–02, a factory Bentley in 2003 and then in privately run R8s in 2004–05. Kristensen had victory snatched from him in 2007 when a wheel came off! He managed to pull off a great victory a year later to beat the faster Peugeot 908s. Kristensen took a record ninth Le Mans victory in 2013, on his way to becoming world champion the same year with Alan McNish and Loïc Duval. Kristensen took an amazing fourteenth podium in his last start the following year to round out an incredible career. But the nine-time winner has not hung up his helmet for good – Kristensen is a regular in historic racing and the Race of Champions.

JACKY ICKX

Le Mans starts: 15

Le Mans wins: 6

Teams raced for:
- Essex Wire Corporation
- John Wyer Automotive
- Scuderia Ferrari
- Gulf Research Racing
- Martini Racing Porsche System
- Essex Motorsport Porsche
- Equipe Liqui Moly – Martini Racing
- Porsche System
- Rothmans Porsche

Jacky Ickx is a Belgian Racing driver, winning eight Formula 1 races and six Le Mans 24 hours. Ickx first raced at Le Mans in 1966 and his first major sports car win coming the same year at Spa. His first of six Le Mans wins came in 1969 in a Ford GT40. To protest the traditional Le Mans start he walked across the track and was last by the end of lap one, but into the last 4 hours, the race became a duel between him and a Porsche. Ickx and Jackie Oliver won by 110 metres making it the closest finish of all time at Le Mans. He next won Le Mans in 1975 and '76 as well as many sports car races. Ickx considers his 1977 Le Mans win the best. He retired from the race early on in another Porsche 936, before he moved to his team mates car. At this stage he was 42nd position. Ickx made up for lost laps through the night and lead by the early morning. His Porsche had a mechanical problem, but the car held on to win the race. He Later won Le Mans in 1981 and 1982 with Derek Bell in the Rothmans 956 Porsche. Ickx made his last Le Mans start in 1985 but was a consultant to the ORECA-run Mazda team in 1991, he is seen as one of the best drivers of all time.

DEREK BELL

Le Mans starts: 26

Le Mans wins: 5

Teams raced for:
- Scuderia Ferrari
- John Wyer Automotive
- Ecurie Francorchamps
- Gulf Racing
- Grand Touring Cars
- Renault Sport
- Porsche System
- Rothmans Porsche
- Richard Lloyd Racing
- Joest Porsche Racing
- ADA Engineering
- Courage Compétition
- Gulf Oil Racing
- David Price Racing

Derek Bell is a British racing driver who won the WSCC twice, the 24 hours of Daytona three times and Le Mans five times. He is also the most successful British driver at Le Mans to date having won the race five times. His first time at Le Mans was in 1970 in a works Ferrari but didn't finish. In 1975 he drove his Gulf Mirage GR8 to victory with Jacky Ickx and won with the Belgian driver in 1981 and 1982. In 1986 and 1987 he teamed up with Hans-Joachim Stuck and Al Holbert to take victory. Driving a Porsche 917 in 1970 he reached the fastest ever speed at Le Mans, 246 mph on the Mulsanne Straight. He has been described by fellow racer Hans-Joachim Stuck as one of the most liked drivers of his generation.

EMANUELE PIRRO

Le Mans starts: 13

Le Mans wins: 5

Teams raced for:
- Martini Racing
- GTC Competition
- Audi Sport Joest
- Champion Racing
- Drayson Racing

Between 1999 and 2007, Emanuele Pirro did not finish off the podium at Le Mans. After a brief Formula 1 career, where the Italian racer only scored three points, Pirro made a switch to touring cars where he won back-to-back Italian Touring car championships in 1994 and 1995. He then won the German Super Tourenwagen Cup in 1996 driving an Audi A4 Quattro. Pirro then joined the Audi Le Mans program in 1999 and came third at Le Mans before three successive Le Mans wins. After a string of third places, Pirro was back on the Le Mans top step in 2006 and 2007. Pirro is now an FIA steward.

FRANK BIELA

Le Mans starts: 10

Le Mans wins: 5

Teams raced for:
- Audi Sport Joest
- Audi Sport UK
- Champion Racing

German race Frank Biela matches Emanuele Pirro and Derek Bell for overall victories with a total of five. Biela has enjoyed a long association with Audi, which began in 1991 in the DTM series, which he won. He then spent several seasons racing in touring car championships, claiming titles in France and Britain, before switching focus to endurance racing. Biela raced the Audi R8R in 1999 at Le Mans, finishing third, before moving across to partner Kristensen and Pirro with the R8. They scored three consecutive wins together from 2000 to 2002, before a DNF in 2003 and finishing fifth in 2004. He returned to the top step in the next two years, alongside Pirro and Marc Werner with the R10 TDI. Biela also won the American Le Mans Series in 2003 and 2005.

CONSTRUCTORS WITH THE MOST ALL TIME WINS

PORSCHE

Le Mans wins: 19

Most consecutive wins: 7

Famous winning cars: 917, 936, 956, 962, 911 GT1, 919 Hybrid

German sports car manufacturer Porsche are the most success-ful team and constructor with nineteen overall victories and more than 100 class wins at Le Mans. The Porsche company was founded in 1931 by Ferdinand Porsche in Stuttgart. The German government wanted a "car for the people" and in 1938 Volkswagen created the very successful Beetle. Porsche adapted this to create their first Porsche badged car, the Type 64 which was launched in 1939. The car was very sleek having been produced in a wind tunnel, it produced about 40 bhp and reached 100 mph top speed. This was the foundation for all Porsches to come. Post-war Germany was very short of supplies but the Porsche company managed to continue and during the 1950s they arguably developed their nicest cars. Quickly Porsche gained a good reputation of producing well balanced fine cars. The cars though were small sports cars which didn't produce much power so motorsport was not an obvious direction to go for the company. The Targa Florio was one of the most dangerous road racing events in the world, first held in 1906, the Italian endurance race proved to be a great opportunity for Porsche to take a class win. But in 1956 they did even better and won the race overall, this was the first eleven wins at the Targa Florio for Porsche. They wanted more motorsport success and to prove the reliability of their cars they first entered Le Mans in 1951. But success was not instant and it took them a record twenty Le Mans starts before they took their first overall win. In 1969 they came so close but lost by 120 metres. The following year Porsche had the best chance of winning with the 917K and they successfully finished 1–2 in very wet conditions. This was the start of the success for Porsche at Le Mans and they managed to win again in 1971 with the longtail version of the 917. Porsche were also dominating the WSCC and won a manufacturer class every year from 1962–1984. They won their third Le Mans in 1976 before Jacky Ickx achieved an amazing comeback victory the following year. Kremer Racing won in 1979 in a 935 and this shows the brilliance of Porsche engineering – if the factory team then didn't win, a privateer team would still have a very good chance to win with Porsche machinery. This was the case through the 1980s and between 1981 and 1987 a mixture of Porsche works cars or the private teams would take victory at Le Mans. With the new LMGT1 regulations in 1994, Porsche saw potential and won with the Dauer 962. Further Le Mans victories followed in '96 and '97 with the WSC-95 car before they took their final win of the decade in 1998 with the 911 LMGT1 version. Porsche didn't compete in prototype sports car racing until 2014 and although they missed out on Le Mans with a technical issue, the 919 hybrid was a great car. The following year the car took a 1–2 result and the WEC. In 2016 Le Mans victory looked to be slipping away but starting the last lap the leading Toyota broke down and Porsche took their eighteenth win. Porsche made it a hat-trick of Le Mans wins the following year and pulled out of WEC at the end of the season. But with the dawn of Hypercar Porsche have announced they will be back aiming for a twentieth victory.

AUDI

Le Mans wins: 13

Most consecutive wins: 5

Famous winning cars: R8, R10, R15, R18

German Car manufacturer Audi started racing prototype sports-cars in 1999, debuting at Le Mans. Two concept cars were developed and raced in their first season – the Audi R8R and the Audi R8C. The R8R achieved a third-place podium on its racing debut at Le Mans and was the concept which Audi continued to develop into the 2000 season. The factory-supported Joest Racing team won at Le Mans three times in a row with the Audi R8 (2000–2002), driven by Tom Kristensen, Frank Biela and Emanuele Pirro. Having been defeated in 2003 by Bentley, Audi returned to the winner's podium in 2004, with the top three finishers all driving R8s. The following year Audi were victorious, but the era of the R8 had come to an end, with the R10 TDI racing in 2006. The R10 TDI a diesel engine and win on its debut at Le Mans. Audi's winning ways continued in 2007 and 2008 before being humiliated by Peugeot in 2009. Audi fought back the next year winning with the brand new R15 TDI Plus and set a new distance record. In the 24 hours Timo Bernhard, Romain Dumas and Mike Rockenfeller completed 397 laps – 3,362 miles. Audi's success continued with the new closed cockpit R18 in 2011 beating Peugeot by 13.8 seconds in a thrilling race. For 2012 the R18 was the car to beat and took another victory. In 2013 Audi won with Tom Kristensen taking his ninth and final Le Mans victory with Loïc Duval and Allan McNish. The competition was tougher than ever in 2014 with the return of Porsche and the ever-strong Toyota team, Audi didn't arrive as favourites. The challenge got even harder after a crash for Duval in practice, but Audi came out on top after a fantastic race. The next year Audi finished second and third after a tough race. The following year, Audi had a bad race but still managed a third-place finish – after this Audi stopped their endurance program. But, as the new Hypercar era dawns, Audi have announced they will be back and are fully intending to add to their thirteen Le Mans victories.

FERRARI

Le Mans wins: 9

Most consecutive wins: 6

Famous winning cars: 166 MM, 375 Plus, 250P, 275 P

Ferrari is possibly the most iconic brand in the world and their founder, Enzo Ferrari, was passionate about his cars racing at Le Mans. Enzo was himself a driver in the pre-war years and founded Scuderia Ferrari in 1929. The team ran Alfa Romeo cars until 1939 when he left Alfa and decided to create his own car. He set up his headquarters in Maranello in Italy and this is where the team are still based today and the whole town revolves around Ferrari. They took their first of nine Le Mans victories in 1949 having had success at the Mille Miglia, which they won a total of eight times. When the WSCC was established in 1953, the Ferrari team were already well established but Enzo was starting to run out of money. So, to fund his racing project he decided to create road going sports cars. The Italian cars were always technologically advanced and during the late 1950s and early '60s, Ferrari were on top form winning six Le Mans in a row. However, after their 1965 victory (which was a privately entered Ferrari) they never won Le Mans overall ever again. However, this could change in the coming years as they have announced they will compete in the new Hypercar Le Mans class. In recent years Ferrari have been Le Mans winners in the GTE PRO class with a full factory effort of 458 and 488 cars. Ferrari have a total of four GTE PRO Le Mans victories: 2012, 2014, 2019 and 2021 as well as success in the previous GT categories. Ferrari have always been loved by spectators especially with their Formula 1 success having competed in the championship since its very first year, 1950. With over 1,000 F1 starts and sixteen constructors' championships to date, Ferrari are possibly the greatest race team of all time.

JAGUAR

Le Mans wins: 7

Most consecutive wins: 3

Famous winning cars: XJ-120C, C-Type, D-Type, XJR-9

The British car maker founded as a sidecar company called Swallow Sidecar also known as SS cars until they changed their name to Jaguar in 1945. William Lyons, founder of Jaguar, knew success at Le Mans could improve car sales. They made a strong start at Le Mans in 1950, Jaguar created the C-Type in 1951 and won with Peter Walker and Peter Whitehead driving. The following year Tony Rolt and Duncan Hamilton repeated the victory. Jaguar's next victory at Le Mans came in 1955, despite the famous tragedy of that race, Mike Hawthorn and Ivor Bueb took victory in the new D-Type. The D-Type remained victorious for the next two years. In the early 1980s Jaguar hit a slump, they needed to restore their reputation and in 1987 they won the WSCC in the 7.0-Litre V12 XJR-9. The following year they managed to win Le Mans, 2 minutes and 36 seconds ahead of Porsche. They missed victory in 1989 but came back strong in 1990 winning in a tough race before pulling out of Le Mans and Sportscar racing.

BENTLEY

Le Mans wins: 6

Most consecutive wins: 4

Famous winning cars: 3 litre Speed, Speed six, Speed 8

Founder of Bentley Motors, W.O. Bentley decided not to enter a works Bentley in 1923, but he attended the race and saw John Duff and Frank Clement finish fourth in a private Bentley 3 Litre Sport. The next year the same two drivers won for the first time in a Bentley. 1927 was the next time Bentley stood on the top step at Le Mans and continued a winning streak for the next three years. After their victory in 1930 Bentley pulled out of the race. After their success at Le Mans road car sales went up for Bentley before the Second World War, they did not compete at Le Mans again until 2001. After a gap of sixty-eight years the British team returned to Le Mans for a planned three-year operation with the EXP Speed 8 in the closed-cockpit LMGTP class. With a twin-turbo 4 litre V8 engine the car was not at all quiet. In their first year returning to Le Mans team Bentley managed a third place overall and a class win. In 2002 they came fourth overall before winning the race out right in 2003 with Tom Kristensen, Rinaldo Capello and Guy Smith driving. That year was a 1–2 for Bentley before pulling out of endurance racing.

TOYOTA

Le Mans wins: 5

Most consecutive wins: 5

Famous winning cars: TS050

Toyota first entered Le Mans in 1985 and have been one of the most unlucky teams in sports car racing. The Japanese manufacturer entered its first Le Mans in the Group C era and finished twelfth in their first race at Circuit de la Sarthe. This also marked the first time a Japanese car had finished the Le Mans 24 hours. The following year neither car finished but the team caried on and in 1990 entered a full season of the WSCC. A sixth place at Le Mans was a good result. 1992 was another step forward for the team with their new and improved TS010 and a first Le Mans podium. But a string of bad luck followed. In 1994 Toyota seemed to have race won but they lost it in the final hour due to a gear linkage issue and finished second. 1998 was Toyota's next big chance to take victory and were running in second place until transmission failure in the final hour put them out of the race. A year later in the crazy 1999 race, Toyota had another great chance and going into the afternoon it was a straight fight for victory between the GT-One Toyota and the BMW. The

GT-One was catching the slower but more efficient BMW, but a tyre blowout stopped any hope of victory. After the GT1 regulations changed, Toyota stopped racing in sports cars until 2012. On their return the they managed to finish second to Audi. 2014 was another disappointment, the car could arguably have won with its 1,000 bhp motor, but third place would have to do. The 2015 car was not as efficient as its rivals, but in 2016 they had the race in their hands. But starting the last lap of the race, the intercooler failed and Porsche won as Toyota were not even classified. In 2018 however nothing was going to stop them as they took a 1–2 result. Since then, they are undefeated at Le Mans and are the team to beat heading into the Hypercar era.

FORD

Le Mans wins: 4

Most consecutive wins: 4

Famous winning cars: GT40, MKII, MKIV

Ford Motor Company is an American car maker founded in 1903 by Henry Ford. In the early sixties Ford decided they needed a new look and decided to buy Ferrari. At the last minute though, Ferrari decided they wanted to sell to Fiat instead. Henry Ford II said, "We are going to race him and beat him at Le Mans." This led to the creation of the GT40. Developed by Carroll Shelby and Ken Miles the car won in 1966 with Bruce McLaren and Chris Amon at the wheel. Ferrari were defeated and Ford won again in 1967, this time in an all-American car with an all-American driver line-up, A. J. Foyt and Dan Gurney – a first for Le Mans. After this Henry Ford II pulled out of Le Mans having spent millions on the project. But in 1968 and 1969, the Ford GT was the car to beat, winning with the privately run JW Automotive entry.

GTE PRO RETURN

In 2015 a new version of the GT was launched and at Le Mans the same year, it was announced that Ford would return to the 24 hours of Le Mans in 2016 with a factory-supported, four-car line-up in LM GTE-Pro. Fifty years after their first win at Le Mans, in 2016, Ford beat Ferrari in the LM GTE-PRO class at Le Mans with Sébastien Bourdais, Dirk Müller and Joey Hand driving. The car also won two more WEC races and three IMSA races that year. Ford continued to have great success on both sides of the Atlantic taking multiple class wins in WEC and IMSA. But at the end of 2019 Ford pulled out of endurance racing.

MATRA

Le Mans wins: 3

Most consecutive wins: 3

Famous winning cars: MS670, MS670B, MS670C

French manufacturer Matra made its debut Le Mans appearance in 1966 with their MS620 Group 6 car. Although they did not finish the race, the team stuck with sportscars and in 1968 decided to build their own engine for their cars. Unfortunately, the car caught fire in the pits with 3 hours to go. But it was not until the seventies when success started to come their way. 1970 had one of the wettest starts to a Le Mans in history, but Matra were unable to take advantage. For 1971 the French team chose to focus their racing effort on Formula 1 and not sportscars. But the following year Graham Hill and Henri Pescarolo took first of three consecutive wins at Le Mans for the French team. The following year they topped off the success of Le Mans with also winning the World Sportscar championship. The dominating MS670 took its last Le Mans victory and Sportscar title in 1974 and did not enter Le Mans again.

PEUGEOT

Le Mans wins: 3

Most consecutive wins: 2

Famous winning cars: 905 EVO, 908 HDi FAP

Peugeot are true French heroes of Le Mans, first entered in 1991 with the 905 Group C car. Although the car won its first world sportscar race at Suzuka, it suffered gearbox problems at Le Mans. The team showed to be serious contenders in sportscar racing having finished second to Jaguar in that year's championship. For 1992 a series of modifications were made to the car creating the EVO. After a second place in the opening race of the season at Silverstone, the manufacturer was a dominant force winning the remaining races of the season including Le Mans. The following year Peugeot took their second win at Le Mans with a convincing 1–2–3 result. After the WSCC folded, Peugeot did not race at Le Mans until 2007 with the 908. The car was an engineering masterpiece and beat the Audi team at Le Mans in 2009. After the 2011 race, the Peugeot team decided to pull out of sportscar racing, but with the creation of Hypercar Peugeot will be aiming for a fourth overall Le Mans win with their radical 9X8 which does not feature a rear wing.

HYPERCAR

THE FUTURE OF LE MANS AND SPORTS CAR RACING

In the summer of 2018, the ACO and FIA confirmed a new top-level prototype class known as Hypercar. The new Hypercar category promises to be an exciting replacement to LMP1. The new rules will allow teams more freedom in car design. The rules also appeal to smaller teams and more manufacturers as a full-season budget is estimated to be twenty-five million euros — 75% lower than LMP1. Top manufacturers and Le Mans winners Toyota, Ford, Ferrari, McLaren and Aston Martin instantly registered interest.

While these new regulations were being worked on, lots of various exciting concept pictures were released. The regulations appealed to manufacturers because teams were allowed free upper body and underbody design. The regulations would come into effect in the WEC at the start of the 2021 season. Toyota, defending LMP1 champions, entered an unchanged driver line-up for the start of the Hypercar era. French LMP2 team, Signatech Alpine, entered a modified LMP1 Rebellion for the full WEC season and Le Mans. American former film director Jim Glickenhaus entered two radical new cars under his own name. Meanwhile as the WEC season was getting underway, in America the IMSA championship confirmed that they would follow the new Hypercar regulations from 2022 onwards. The USA specifications would be slightly different to the LMH regulations in Europe. The USA regulations would be known as LMDh (Le Mans Daytona Hybrid), and instantly multiple manufacturers were interested. The idea was that the two championships, IMSA and WEC, would both come together to compete at the Le Mans 24 hours.

Glickenhaus at Le Mans

The first Hypercar WEC race took place in 2021 at Spa Francorchamps, however Glickenhaus were not ready to compete and did not enter the championship until the following race in Portugal. At Spa Toyota took a 1–2 in qualifying but Alpine were not far behind and gained from the #7 Toyota having "an off" in the race. The #8 Toyota won and made history as the first Hypercar winner in international competition. The following race was the 8 hours of Portimão, and Glickenhaus made their racing debut. Although the American team did not hit the headlines with the results, it was a very important weekend for the team to gather data for Le Mans. Alpine took pole for the 8-hour race and managed to build up a lead from the two Toyotas, but the fuel economy of the French car was not as good as the Toyota team. The Alpine had to make one more pitstop taking the race down to the wire, but in the end, it was a 1–2 finish for Toyota with Alpine third. All three cars finished on the lead lap. Meanwhile in the LMP2 category Jota Sport took a one two in qualifying but a first corner incident nearly took them out the race. However, a clever fuel strategy by the British team helped them fight back to the front and after the 8 hours, the 38-car won with drivers Antony Davidson, Roberto González and home hero António Félix da Costa the drivers. The first Hypercar Le Mans took place in 2021 and five cars made up the top class. The start of the race was behind safety car for the first two laps due to the rain before the two-by-two formation start. The #7 Toyota cleared the first turn and the Alpine got up into second place, but behind, at the Dunlop chicane, the #8 Toyota got spun around by the Glickenhaus. The rest of the cars in other classes had to take avoiding action! The #7 car had cleared off into the distance as the Alpine tried to catch up. The #8 Toyota had a slow lap back to the pits after its spin, and the Glickenhaus had front end damage. During the first hours of the race, the track began to dry, and the #8 Toyota managed to get back up to the front of the class. Going into the night, the #7 Toyota was leading with the Alpine and the #8 Toyota battling for second place. Ultimately, the Alpine had relatively bad fuel economy meaning it was Toyota's to lose. By 16 hours in, Toyota were four laps ahead despite a small technical problem during the morning with both cars, the Japanese brand were in control and finished 1–2 overall with a first victory for the #7 in the Hypercar class. Race winner Jose Maria Lopez described the victory as "a dream come true." They were odds on favourite – the only car with four-wheel drive, and the only car with hybrid power, with a budget much bigger than Alpine or Glickenhaus. Alpine managed to finish third and look to be a force to be reckoned with in years to come and are determined to win at their home track. The Glickenhaus performed magnificently at their first Le Mans finishing fourth and fifth. After Le Mans, Toyota ran away with the remaining Hypercar season as the only team with hybrid power. The #7 car driven by Mike Conway, Kamui Kobayashi and José María López took the title ahead of the #8 car. Alpine beat Glickenhaus to take second in the Hypercar manufacturers standings. The Hypercar category showed growth and Peugeot confirmed they would be racing in 2022. But Peugeot were not ready for the first race of the new season and confirmed they would take part in the Monza 6 hours – the race after Le Mans.

The first round of the 2022 season was the 1,000 miles of Sebring a disused airport famous for its bumpy surface which did not suit the Toyota. This left Alpine to dominate the race and take their first win in Hypercar. Toyota fought back at Spa, despite a Glickenhaus pole, to take their first win of the season with the #7 car. The following race was Le Mans and despite the promising pace from Glickenhaus and Alpine in practice, Toyota took a dominating 1–2 in qualifying and right from the start of the race they built up a lead leaving the competition behind. The race was not over though because the two Toyotas were very evenly matched and were constantly battling for the lead. However, early in the morning the leading #7 car stopped at Arnage Corner. The problem was the electronics and they lost nearly 2 minutes fixing the problem. This left the #8 car in the lead to take another victory at Le Mans. The #709 Glickenhaus managed to stay out of trouble to finish third unlike their #708 car. The Alpine struggled with various bits of bad luck and spent most of the time yo-yoing up and down the LMP2 order, eventually they finished twenty-third overall.

After Le Mans, Peugeot made their Hypercar debut with the 9X8. The car has an unusual design because it has no back wing and the French team believed that the car still produced enough downforce without one. The race was at Monza and proved to be very eventful as Glickenhaus took pole. The American team led, and the car was very quick, however the engine didn't last the whole race. Toyota and Alpine battled for the win and the race was very close, but Alpine managed to take their second victory of the season by just 2.7 seconds ahead of Toyota. Peugeot had a tough but promising race with one car finishing, and both showed good pace.

After this race the Hypercar class really began to take shape with Porsche announcing its car called the 963 for the 2023 season and the list of drivers to compete. Within days of this announcement, British LMP2 team Jota Sport announced that they would be entering a private 963 into the WEC for 2023. BMW had previously announced they would return to sportscar racing and just before Le Mans unveiled their LMDh car as well Cadillac and Acura confirming they will also be in the class for 2023. There had been speculation of Alpine and Lamborghini joining, and they both separately confirmed this as well as a chassis provider for their team ahead of the 2024 season. One of the biggest names in motorsport, Ferrari, confirmed that they would be making a Prototype class return and aiming to win Le Mans for the first time since 1965 as well as exciting news that Vanwall and ByKolles would be merging and entering Hypercar soon.

So, all this means that the 2023 Le Mans is set to be possibly the most competitive in history and this proves that Le Mans is still the best place for exciting motorsport. Over its 100-year history it has attracted so much attention from Hollywood, movie stars like Steve McQueen and Paul Newman as well as racing drivers from other motorsport categories such Sébastien Loeb, Fernando Alonso and Nigel Mansell with his two sons Leo and Greg. Le Mans has seen so many great rivalries and is a place where drivers become legends. The race has helped improve technology and overall has made road cars safer for people every day. Le Mans has been seen as a great place by manufacturers to prove that their cars and technology are the best in the world and overall, this is how the event started – a way to prove that the motorcar was sporty yet reliable. Over the entire history of the race, we have seen so many beautiful cars compete over so many eras such as Group 5, Group C, GT1 and LMP1. The race has helped shaped the motorcar and is arguably the best sporting spectacle in the world with on average over 250,000 spectators attending the race as well as millions watching on TV worldwide. With the Hypercar era ever expanding, nobody is quite sure what the future will hold and what on track battles are to come. One thing we can be sure of is that it will be absolutely fantastic!

RECORDS AND STATS

Most total wins for a constructor		
Wins	**Constructor**	**Year**
19	Porsche	1970, 1971, 1976, 1977, 1979, 1981–1987, 1994, 1996-1998, 2015–2017
13	Audi	2000–2002, 2004–2008, 2010–2014
9	Ferrari	1949, 1954, 1958, 1960–1965
7	Jaguar	1951, 1953, 1955–1957, 1988, 1990
6	Bentley	1924, 1927–1930, 2003
5	Toyota	2018–2022
4	Alfa Romeo	1931–1934
	Ford	1966–1969
3	Matra-Simca	1972–1974
	Peugeot	1992, 1993, 2009
2	Lorraine-Dietrich	1925, 1926
	Bugatti	1937, 1939

Most total wins for a constructor		
Wins	**Constructor**	**Year**
1	Chenard-Walcker	1923
	Lagonda	1935
	Delahaye	1938
	Talbot-Lago	1950
	Mercedes-Benz	1952
	Aston Martin	1959
	Mirage	1975
	Renault-Alpine	1978
	Rondeau	1980
	Sauber-Mercedes	1989
	Mazda	1991
	McLaren	1995
	BMW	1999

Most wins by team		
Wins	**Team**	**Year**
13	Joest Racing	1984–1985, 1996–1997, 2000–2002, 2006, 2010–2014
12	Porsche	1976–1977, 1981–1983, 1986–1987, 1994, 1998, 2015–2017
7	Scuderia Ferrari	1954, 1958, 1960–1964
5	Jaguar	1951, 1953, 1955, 1988, 1990
	Toyota Gazoo Racing	2018–2022
4	Bentley Motors Ltd.	1927–1930
3	Matra Sports	1972–1974
	Peugeot Sport	1992–1993, 2009

Most wins by team		
Wins	**Team**	**Year**
2	Ecurie Ecosse	1956–1957
	Shelby American Inc.	1966–1967
	John Wyer Automotive Engineering	1968–1969

Most consecutive wins for a constructor		
Wins	**Constructor**	**Consecutive wins**
7	Porsche	1981–1987
6	Ferrari	1960–1965
5	Audi	2004–2008
	Audi	2010–2014
	Toyota	2018–2022
4	Bentley	1927–1930
	Alfa Romeo	1931–1934
	Ford	1966–1969

Most wins by cars		
Wins	**Car**	**Year**
5	Audi R8	2000–2002, 2004, 2005
4	Alfa Romeo 8C 2300	1931–1934
	Ford GT40	1966–1969
	Porsche 956	1982–1985
	Audi R18	2011–2014
3	Jaguar D-Type	1955–1957
	Ferrari 250 TR	1958, 1960, 1961
	Matra-Simca MS670	1972–1974
	Porsche 936	1976, 1977, 1981
	Audi R10 TDI	2006– 2008
	Porsche 919 Hybrid	2015–2017
	Toyota TS050 Hybrid	2018–2020
2	Lorraine-Dietrich B3-6	1925, 1926
	Bentley Speed Six	1929, 1930
	Bugatti Type 57	1937, 1939
	Porsche 917K	1970, 1971
	Porsche 962C	1986, 1987
	Peugeot 905	1992, 1993
	Porsche WSC-95	1996, 1997
	Toyota GR010 Hybrid	2021, 2022

Most consecutive wins by specific cars		
Wins	**Car with serial number**	**Year**
2	Bentley Speed Six #LB2332	1929, 1930
	Ferrari 250 P/275 P #0816	1963, 1964
	Ford GT40 #P-1075	1968, 1969
	Porsche 956 #117	1984, 1985
	TWR Porsche WSC-95 #691	1996, 1997

Other constructor records		
Description	**Record**	**Details**
Wins		
Most class wins	108	Porsche
Most class wins in a single race	5	Porsche in 1981 and 1982
Podiums		
Most 1–2 finishes	12	Porsche in 1970, 1971, 1979, 1982–1987, 1996, 1998, 2015
Most podiums	54	Porsche
Most podium lockouts	8	Porsche in 1970, 1979, 1982–1986, 1996
Most consecutive podiums	18	Audi between 1999 and 2016
Most podiums before first win	6	Toyota
Most podiums without winning	3	Pescarolo
Starts		
Most participations by a single constructor	72	Porsche between 1951 and 2022
Most entries by a single constructor (total)	850	Porsche since 1951

Other constructor records		
Description	**Record**	**Details**
Most participations without a class win	15	Dome
Fewest starts before first win	1st start	Chenard-Walcker (1923) Ferrari (1949) McLaren (1995)
Most starts before first win	20th start	Porsche, Toyota
Pole positions		
Most consecutive pole positions	6	Porsche between 1978 and 1983 Toyota between 2017 and 2022

Most total wins for a driver		
Wins	Drivers	Years
9	Tom Kristensen	1997, 2000–2005, 2008, 2013
6	Jacky Ickx	1969, 1975–1977, 1981–1982
5	Derek Bell	1975, 1981, 1982, 1986, 1987
	Frank Biela	2000–2002, 2006, 2007
	Emanuele Pirro	2000–2002, 2006, 2007
4	Olivier Gendebien	1958, 1960–1962
	Henri Pescarolo	1972–1974, 1984
	Yannick Dalmas	1992, 1994, 1995, 1999
	Sebastien Buemi	2018–2020, 2022
3	Woolf Barnato	1928–1930
	Luigi Chinetti	1932, 1934, 1949
	Phil Hill	1958, 1961, 1962
	Hurley Haywood	1977, 1983, 1994
	Klaus Ludwig	1979, 1984, 1985
	Al Holbert	1983, 1986, 1987
	Rinaldo Capello	2003, 2004, 2008
	Marco Werner	2005–2007
	Allan McNish	1998, 2008, 2013
	André Lotterer	2011, 2012, 2014
	Marcel Fässler	2011, 2012, 2014
	Benoît Tréluyer	2011, 2012, 2014
	Kazuki Nakajima	2018–2020
	Brendon Hartley	2017, 2020, 2022

Drivers who won their first entries	
Driver	**Year**
André Lagache	1923
René Léonard	1923
Bernard Rubin	1928
Woolf Barnato	1928
Luigi Chinetti	1932
Tazio Nuvolari	1933
Philippe Etancelin	1934
Luis Fontés	1935
Jean-Pierre Wimille	1937
Peter Walker	1951
Fritz Riess	1952
Hermann Lang	1952
Ivor Bueb	1955
A. J. Foyt	1967
Hurley Haywood	1977
Andy Wallace	1988
Christophe Bouchut	1993
Éric Hélary	1993
Alexander Wurz	1996
Tom Kristensen	1997
Laurent Aïello	1998
Nico Hülkenberg	2015
Earl Bamber	2015
Fernando Alonso	2018

Most total starts for a driver	
Driver	**Starts**
Henri Pescarolo	33
Bob Wollek	30
Yojiro Terada	29
Derek Bell	26
François Migault	24
Jan Lammers	
Emmanuel Collard	
Claude Ballot-Lena	23
Olivier Beretta	
Claude Haldi	22
Pierre Yver	
Jan Magnussen	

Drivers who have won in all of their entries		
Number of entries and wins	**Driver**	**Year**
3	Woolf Barnato	1928–1930
2	Jean-Pierre Wimille	1937, 1939
	Fernando Alonso	2018, 2019
1	Luis Fontés	1935
	Hermann Lang	1952
	A. J. Foyt	1967
	Tazio Nuvolari	1933
	Nico Hülkenberg	2015

Other driver records		
Description	**Record**	**Details**
Wins		
Youngest winner overall	22 years, 91 days	Alexander Wurz in 1996
Youngest winner by class	18 years, 352 days	Julien Andlauer in 2018 (LM GTE-Am category)
Oldest winner	47 years, 343 days	Luigi Chinetti in 1949
Most time between successive wins	13 years	Alexander Wurz (1996 – 2009)
Most time between first and last wins	17 years	Hurley Haywood (1977 – 1994)
Most starts before first win	16th start	David Brabham in 2009
Lowest start position before win	16th	Hans Herrmann and Richard Attwood in 1970
Starts and finishes		
Youngest driver to start	16 years 119 days	Josh Pierson (2022)
Oldest driver to start	75 years 269 days	Dominique Bastien (2021)
Most consecutive starts	30	Henri Pescarolo (1970 – 1999)
Most consecutive finishes	11	Johnny O'Connell (1999 – 2009)
Most races between first and last start	36	Jan Lammers (1983 – 2018)
Most starts without winning overall	30	Bob Wollek
Most time in the car during 24 hours	24 hours	Edward Ramsden Hall in 1950

Other driver records		
Description	**Record**	**Details**
Most time in the car during 24 hours for a winner	23 hours 15 minutes 17 seconds	Louis Rosier in 1950
Most entries with different constructors	16	François Migault
Most entries with the same constructor	20	Bob Wollek with Porsche (1975–1983, 1986–1990,1993, 1996–2000)
Most entries as teammates	14	Tracy Krohn and Niclas Jönsson (2006–2019)
Most finishes	19	Derek Bell
Most retirements	18	Henri Pescarolo

Other driver records		
Podiums		
Most podiums	14	Tom Kristensen
Most podiums without a win overall	6	Bob Wollek
Most consecutive podium finishes	9	Emanuele Pirro (1999–2007)
Youngest driver on the podium overall	18 years, 133 days	Ricardo Rodriguez (2nd in 1960)
Oldest driver on the podium overall	55 years, 110 days	Mario Andretti (2nd in 1995)
Oldest driver on the podium by class	68 years, 111 days	Jack Gerber (3rd in 2013 in the LMGTE-Am category)
Biggest gap between first and last podiums overall	19 years, 361 days	Bob Wollek (1978–1998)
Most races without a podium overall	29	Yojiro Terada

Other driver records

Pole positions

Most total pole positions	5	Jacky Ickx (1975, 1978, 1981, 1982, 1983)
Most race wins from pole position	3	Jacky Ickx (1975, 1981, 1982)
Most pole positions without winning	3	Bob Wollek (1979, 1984, 1987) Stéphane Sarrazin (2007-2009)
Youngest polesitter	23 years, 146 days	Pedro Rodríguez (1963)
Oldest polesitter	43 years, 220 days	Bob Wollek (1987)

Fastest laps

Most total fastest laps	5	Jacky Ickx (1977, 1979, 1980,1983, 1985)
Most consecutive fastest laps	4	Mike Hawthorn (1955–1958)
Youngest driver to set fastest lap	19 years, 114 days	Ricardo Rodriguez (1961)
Oldest driver to set fastest lap	51 years, 44 days	Francis Curzon (1935)

Race Records

Description	Record	Details
Longest distance covered	5410.713 km (397 laps)	Audi R15+ TDI in 2010
Most laps completed	397	1971 & 2010
Fastest lap (since 1990, pole position)	3:14.791	Kamui Kobayashi in a Toyota TS050 Hybrid in 2017
Fastest lap (until 1989, pole position)	3:13.90	Pedro Rodríguez in a Porsche 917 in 1971
Smallest winning margin	20 metres	1966

Race Records		
Description	**Record**	**Details**
Largest winning margin	349.808 km	In 1927 between a Bentley and a Salmson
Highest average race speed by a winner	225.228 km/h (140 mph)	Audi R15+ TDI in 2010
Highest average lap speed (qualifying)	251.881 km/h (157 mph)	Kamui Kobayashi with a Toyota TS050 Hybrid in 2017
Highest average lap speed (Race)	248.628 km/h (154 mph)	Mike Conway with a Toyota TS05 Hybrid in 2019
Highest top speed	407 km/h (253 mph)	Roger Dorchy with a WM P88-Peugeot in 1988
Most cars in a single race	62	In 2022
Fewest cars in a single race	17	In 1930
Most finishers	53	In 2022
Fewest finishers	6	In 1931
Lowest percentage of finishers	13.7%	In 1970 (7/51 finishers)
Most cars in the leading lap	2	In 1933, 1935, 1966, 1969, 1983, 1987, 1988, 2004, 2008, 2011, 2019 and 2022
Highest attendance	400,000	In 1969
Lowest attendance	0	In 2020

Most wins by fuel type		
Wins	**Fuel**	**Year**
73	Petrol	1923–2005
8	Petrol-electric hybrid	2015–2022
6	Diesel	2006–2011
3	Diesel-electric hybrid	2012–2014

Wins by tyre supplier		
Wins	**Manufacturer**	**Year**
34	Dunlop	1924–1931, 1935, 1937–1939, 1950, 1951, 1953, 1955–1957, 1960–1964, 1977, 1979, 1981–1988, 1991
31	Michelin	1923, 1978, 1989, 1992, 1993, 1995, 1998–2022
14	Goodyear	1965–1967, 1970, 1972–1976, 1980, 1990, 1994, 1996, 1997
5	Englebert	1932–1934, 1949, 1958
3	Firestone	1968, 1969, 1971
1	Continental	1952
	Pirelli	1954
	Avon	1959

WINNERS

Overall Winners		
Year	**Car**	**Drivers**
1923	Chenard-Walker 3 Litre Sport	Andre Lagache, Rene Leonard
1924	Bentley 3 Litre Sport Vanden Plas Tourer	John Duff, Frank Clement
1925	Lorraine-Dietrich B3-6 Le Mans	Gerard de Courcelles, Andre Rossignol
1926	Lorraine-Dietrich B3-6 Le Mans	Robert Bloc, Andre Rossignol
1927	Bentley 3 Litre Sport Vanden Plas Tourer	John Dudley Benjafield, Sammy Davis
1928	Bentley 4.5 Litre	Woolf Barnato, Bernard Rubin
1929	Bentley Speed Six Works Team Car	Woolf Barnato, Henry Birkin
1930	Bentley Speed Six Works Team Car	Woolf Barnato, Glen Kidston
1931	Alfa Romeo 8C 2300 Zagato Le Mans	Lord Howe, Henry Birkin
1932	Alfa Romeo 8C 2300 Figoni Spider	Raymond Sommer, Luigi Chinetti
1933	Alfa Romeo 8C 2300 Zagato Spider	Tazio Nuvolari, Raymond Sommer
1934	Alfa Romeo 8C 2300 Brianza Le Mans Spider	Philippe Etancelin, Luigi Chinetti
1935	Lagonda M45R	Johnny Hindmarsh, Louis Fontes
1937	Bugatti Type 57 G Tank	Jean-Pierre Wimille, Robert Benoist

Overall Winners		
Year	Car	Drivers
1938	Delahaye 135 S Competition Roadster	Eugene Chaboud, Jean Tremoulet
1939	Bugatti Type 57 C	Jean-Pierre Wimille, Pierre Veyron
1949	Ferrari 166 MM Touring Barchetta	Lord Selsdon, Luigi Chinetti
1950	Talbot Lago T26C Biplace Sport	Louis Rosier, Jean Louis Rosier
1951	Jaguar C-Type	Peter Walker, Peter Whitehead
1952	Mercedes-Benz 300 SL Competition Coupe	Hermann Lang, Fritz Riess
1953	Jaguar C-Type Lightweight	Tony Rolt, Duncan Hamilton
1954	Ferrari 375 Plus Pinin Farina Spyder	Jose Froilan Gonzales, Maurice Trintignant
1955	Jaguar D-Type Works Long Nose	Mike Hawthorn, Ivor Bueb
1956	Jaguar D-Type	Ron Flockhart, Ninian Sanderson
1957	Jaguar D-Type Works Long Nose	Ron Flockhart, Ivor Bueb
1958	Ferrari 250 TR58	Phil Hill, Olivier Gendebien
1959	Aston Martin DBR1	Carroll Shelby, Roy Salvadori
1960	Ferrari 250 TR59/60	Paul Frere, Olivier Gendebien
1961	Ferrari 250 TRI61	Phil Hill, Olivier Gendebien
1962	Ferrari 330 TRI/LM	Phil Hill, Olivier Gendebien
1963	Ferrari 250 P	Ludovico Scarfiotti, Lorenzo Bandini
1964	Ferrari 275 P	Jean Guichet, Nino Vaccarella
1965	Ferrari 250 LM	Masten Gregory, Jochen Rindt
1966	Ford GT40 Mk II	Chris Amon, Bruce McLaren

Overall Winners		
Year	Car	Drivers
1967	Ford Mk IV	Dan Gurney, A.J. Foyt
1968	Ford GT40 Mk I Gulf	Pedro Rodriguez, Lucien Bianchi
1969	Ford GT40 Mk I Gulf	Jackie Oliver, Jacky Ickx
1970	Porsche 917 K	Hans Herrmann, Richard Attwood
1971	Porsche 917 K	Gijs van Lennep, Helmut Marko
1972	Matra MS670	Henri Pescarolo, Graham Hill
1973	Matra MS670B	Henri Pescarolo, Gerard Larousse
1974	Matra MS670C	Henri Pescarolo, Gerard Larousse
Year	Car	Drivers
1975	Mirage GR8 Cosworth	Derek Bell, Jacky Ickx
1976	Porsche 936	Gijs van Lennep, Jacky Ickx
1977	Porsche 936	Jurgen Barth, Jacky Ickx, Hurley Haywood
1978	Renault-Alpine A442	Didier Pironi, Jean-Pierre Jaussaud
1979	Porsche 935 K3	Klaus Ludwig, Don Whittingdon, Bill Whittingdon
1980	Rondeau M379 Cosworth	Jean Rondeau, Jean-Pierre Jaussaud
1981	Porsche 936	Derek Bell, Jacky Ickx
1982	Porsche 956	Derek Bell, Jacky Ickx
1983	Porsche 956	Al Holbert, Vern Schuppan, Hurley Haywood
1984	Porsche 956	Henri Pescarolo, Klaus Ludwig
1985	Porsche 956	Paolo Barilla, Klaus Ludwig, John 'Winter'

Overall Winners		
Year	Car	Drivers
1986	Porsche 962C	Derek Bell, Al Holbert, Hans-Joachim Stuck
1987	Porsche 962C	Derek Bell, Al Holbert, Hans-Joachim Stuck
1988	Jaguar XJR-9 LM	Andy Wallace, John Dumfries, Jan Lammers
1989	Sauber Mercedes C9	Jochen Mass, Manuel Reuter, Stanley Dickens
1990	Jaguar XJR-12	Martin Brundle, John Nielsen, Price Cobb
1991	Mazda 787B	Bertrand Cachot, Johnny Herbert, Volker Weidler
1992	Peugeot 905 Evo 1 Bis	Derek Warwick, Yannick Dalmas, Martin Blundell
1993	Peugeot 905 Evo 1 Bis	Geoff Brabham, Christophe Bouchut, Éric Hélary
1994	Dauer 962 LM Sport	Mauro Baldi, Yannick Dalmas, Hurley Haywood
1995	McLaren F1 GTR	J.J. Lehto, Yannick Dalmas, Masanori Sekiya
1996	Porsche TWR WSC95	Manuel Reuter, Davy Jones, Alexander Wurz
1997	Porsche TWR WSC95	Michele Alboreto, Tom Kristensen, Stefan Johansson
1998	Porsche 911 GT1 '98	Allan McNish, Laurent Aiello, Stephane Ortelli
1999	BMW V12 LMR	Joachim Winkelhock, Yannick Dalmas, Pierluigi Martini
2000	Audi R8	Frank Biela, Tom Kristensen, Emanuele Pirro

Overall Winners		
Year	**Car**	**Drivers**
2001	Audi R8	Frank Biela, Tom Kristensen, Emanuele Pirro
2002	Audi R8	Frank Biela, Tom Kristensen, Emanuele Pirro
2003	Bentley Speed 8	Guy Smith, Tom Kristensen, Rinaldo Capello
2004	Audi R8	Seiji Ara, Tom Kristensen, Rinaldo Capello
2005	Audi R8	J.J. Lehto, Tom Kristensen, Marco Werner
2006	Audi R10 TDI	Frank Biela, Emanuele Pirro, Marco Werner
2007	Audi R10 TDI	Frank Biela, Emanuele Pirro, Marco Werner
2008	Audi R10 TDI	Allan McNish, Tom Kristensen, Rinaldo Capello
2009	Peugeot 908 HDi FAP	David Brabham, Marc Gene, Alexander Wurz
2010	Audi R15 plus TDI	Timo Bernhard, Romain Dumas, Mike Rockenfeller
2011	Audi R18 TDI	Benoit Tréluyer, Andre Lotterer, Marcel Fässler
2012	Audi R18 e-tron quattro	Benoit Tréluyer, Andre Lotterer, Marcel Fässler
2013	Audi R18 e-tron quattro	Allan McNish, Tom Kristensen, Loïc Duval
2014	Audi R18 e-tron quattro	Benoit Tréluyer, Andre Lotterer, Marcel Fässler
2015	Porsche 919 Hybrid	Nick Tandy, Nico Hülkenberg, Earl Bamber
2016	Porsche 919 Hybrid	Romain Dumas, Neel Jani, Marc Lieb

Overall Winners		
Year	**Car**	**Drivers**
2017	Porsche 919 Hybrid	Earl Bamber, Timo Bernhard, Brendon Hartley
2018	Toyota TS050 Hybrid	Fernando Alonso, Sébastien Buemi, Kazuki Nakajima
2019	Toyota TS050 Hybrid	Fernando Alonso, Sébastien Buemi, Kazuki Nakajima
2020	Toyota TS050 Hybrid	Sébastien Buemi, Brendon Hartley, Kazuki Nakajima
2021	Toyota GR010 Hybrid	Mike Conway, Kamui Kobayashi, José María López
2022	Toyota GR010 Hybrid	Sébastien Buemi , Brendon Hartley, Ryō Hirakawa

Index

Introduction

Photo 1 Le Mans typography: artwork by David Taylor.

The First Le Mans: 1923

Photo 2 1923 race: Car Endurance Race 1923, "24 Heures de Mans". Author D.A.S. (Germany), File:LeMans 1923.jpg - Wikimedia Commons, 22 September 2006, Public Domain

Photo 3 1923 trophy: The triennial Rudge-Whitworth Cup of the 24 Hours of Le Mans, created in 1923. Author L'Auto-vélo, File:La Coupe triennale Rudge-Whitworth des 24 heures du Mans, créée en 1923.jpg - Wikimedia Commons, 10 October 2017, Public Domain

Photo 4 1923 winner: Winner of the first Le Mans proper in 1923. Author David Merrett, File:Chenard & Walcker Sport.jpg - Wikimedia Commons, 3 March 2010, Creative Commons Attribution 2.0 Generic license.

Circuit de la Sarthe

Photo 5 circuit de la Sarthe: artwork by David Taylor

Photo 6 Track icon: artwork by David Taylor

Photo 7 Pit lane: Main Grandstand and Race control at Le Mans 1995. Author Martin Lee, File:Main Grandstand and Race control at Le Mans 1995 (49627443572).jpg - Wikimedia Commons, 4 March 2020, Creative Commons Attribution 2.0 Generic license.

Photo 8 Dunlop map: artwork by David Taylor

Photo 9 Dunlop curve: Le Mans 24 Hours 2017. Author David Merrett, File:Two Ferrari 488 GTEs, a Ford GT and a Chevrolet Corvette C7R (36119446806).jpg - Wikimedia Commons, 17 June 2017, Creative Commons Attribution 2.0 Generic license.

Photo 10 Dunlop chicane: Mercede-Benz CLR heads under Dunlop Bridge at the1999 Le Mans. Author Martin Lee, File:Mercede-Benz CLR heads under Dunlop Bridge at the1999 Le Mans (51911409198).jpg - Wikimedia Commons, 23 February 2022, Creative Commons Attribution 2.0 Generic license.

Photo 11 Esses map: artwork by David Taylor

Photo 12 Esses 1995: McLaren F1 GTR - Olivier Grouillard, Derek Bell & Andy Wallace on the run down from Dunlop Bridge to the Esses at the 1996 Le Mans. Author Martin Lee, File:Mclaren F1 GTR - Olivier Grouillard, Derek Bell & Andy Wallace on the run down from Dunlop Bridge to the Esses at the 1996 Le Mans (51718391754).jpg - Wikimedia Commons, 25 November 2021, Creative Commons Attribution 2.0 Generic license.

Photo 13 Tertre rouge map: artwork by David Taylor

Photo 14 Tertre rouge corner: Tertre Rouge Le Mans at night. Author florenzkalvarec, File:Terte Rouge at night 2008.jpg - Wikimedia Commons, 12 July 2008, Creative Commons Attribution 2.0 Generic license.

Photo 15 Mulsanne straight: TOP: Route Nationale 138 road. Author Pete, File:Mulsanne Le Mans.jpg - Wikimedia Commons, 18 June 2006. MIDLE: United Autosports at 2019 Le Mans test, File:United-autosports-le-mans-test-087.jpg - Wikimedia Commons, 2 June 2019. BOTTOM: Matra Simca MS 670 B N°12 Equipe Matra Simca Shell Technique, File:24H du Mans 1973 (5089637955).jpg - Wikimedia Commons, 10 June 1973, Creative Commons Attribution 2.0 Generic license.

Photo 16 From Mulsanne Corner to Indianapolis map: artwork by David Taylor

Photo 17 From Mulsanne Corner to Indianapolis: United Autosport lors des 24 Heures du Mans 2017. Author United Autosports, File:United Autosports Road to Le Mans 2017-21 (35271421836).jpg - Wikimedia Commons, 14 June 2017, Creative Commons Attribution 2.0 Generic license.

Photo 18 Arnage map: artwork by David Taylor

Photo 19 Arnage: Dauer 962 LM - Hans-Joachim Stuck, Thierry Boutsen & Danny Sullivan exits Arnage followed by Venturi 400 - Stephane Ratel, Franz Hunkeler & Edouard Chaufour at the 1994 Le Mans. Author Martin Lee, File:Dauer 962 LM - Hans-Joachim Stuck, Thierry Boutsen & Danny Sullivan exits Arnage followed by Venturi 400 - Stephane Ratel, Franz Hunkeler & Edouard Chaufour at the 1994 Le Mans (31933499156).jpg - Wikimedia Commons, 7 January 2008, Creative Commons Attribution 2.0 Generic license.

Photo 20 Photo 20 From Arnage to the Porsche Curves map: artwork by David Taylor

Photo 21 Porsche curves map: artwork by David Taylor

Photo 22 Ford chicane map: artwork by David Taylor

Photo 23 Ford chicane: The Ford Chicanes and garage complex of the Circuit de la Sarthe viewed during qualifying for the 2009 24 Hours of Le Mans. Author Mike Roberts, File:Le Mans From Above.jpg - Wikimedia Commons, 11 June 2009, Creative Commons Attribution 2.0 Generic license.

Photo 24 track changes: artwork by David Taylor

The First Years: 1924 -1939

Photo 25 1928: Bentley #4 of Barnato and Rubin at the 1928 24 Hours of Le Mans. Author Agence de presse Meurisse, File:Bentley 4 of Barnato and Rubin at the 1928 24 Hours of Le Mans.jpg - Wikimedia Commons, 16 June 1928, Public Domain

Photo 26 1929: Start Lasarte GP Guipúzcoa. Author Fondo Foto Car. Ricardo Martín, File:Lasarte GP Guipúzcoa 1929-07-28-1111780 o.jpg - Wikimedia Commons, 28 July 1929, Creative Commons Attribution-Share Alike 3.0 license.

Photo 27 1929: Bentley #10 of Benjafield and d'Erlanger at the 1929 24 Hours of Le Mans. Author Agence de presse Meurisse, File:Bentley 10 of Benjafield and d'Erlanger at the 1929 24 Hours of Le Mans.jpg - Wikimedia Commons, 15 June 1929, Public Domain

Photo 28 1933: 1933 24 Hours of Le Mans, at the Eastern Bend. Author Le Journal, File:24 Heures du Mans 1933, au virage de l'Est.jpg - Wikimedia Commons, 19 June 1933, Public Domain

Photo 29 1939: The 1939 24 Hours of Le Mans. Author Le Populaire, File:Les 24 Heures du Mans 1939.jpg - Wikimedia Commons, 23 April 2017, Public Domain

Traditions

Photo 30 Time table: artwork by David Taylor

Photo 31 Radio: artwork by David Taylor

Photo 32 winners handprints: Bronze plaque of the footprints of the winners of the 2009 24 hours. Author OldLion, File:Hall of fame Le Mans-winners 2009.JPG - Wikimedia Commons, 7 April 2016, Creative Commons Attribution-Share Alike 4.0 International license.

Danger: 1949 – 1959

Photo 33 1955: Image from an amateur 16mm film, showing the take-off of the Mercedes 300 SLR at the 24 Hours of Le Mans 1955, after colliding with the Austin-Healey 100S. Author FlyAkwa, File:Décollage de la Mercedes-Benz 300 SLR au Mans 1955.png - Wikimedia Commons, 11 June 1955, Creative Commons Attribution-Share Alike 4.0 International license.

Photo 34 1955 News Paper: artwork by David Taylor, 12 Jun 1955, 1 - Daily News at Newspapers.com. Public Domain

Photo 35 Aston Martin 1959: Aston Martin DBR1/1 driven by Carroll Shelby. Author C5813, File:1958-03-28 Sebring Aston DBR1-1 Shelby.jpg - Wikimedia Commons, 22 March 1958, Creative Commons Attribution-Share Alike 4.0 International license.

Rivalry and Revenge: 1960 – 1969

Photo 36 (full page background picture): Kind permission from Exoto

Photo 37 1969 start: LE DEPART. Author ZANTAFIO56, File:24 heures du MANS 1969 (4985489011).jpg - Wikimedia Commons, 14 June 1969, Creative Commons Attribution 2.0 Generic license.

Photo 38 1969: LE DEPART. Author ZANTAFIO56, File:24 heures du MANS 1969 (4986102240).jpg - Wikimedia Commons, 14 June 1969, Creative Commons Attribution 2.0 Generic license.

Photo 39 1969: TOP: 24 Heures du MANS 1969. File:24 Heures du MANS 1969 (4986047927).jpg - Wikimedia Commons. BOTTOM: Ford GT 40 N°6 John Wyer Automotive Engineering Technique, Author ZANTAFIO56,15 June 1969, Creative Commons Attribution 2.0 Generic license.

Group 5 and Group 6: 1970 – 1979

Photo 40 1970: Porsche 917 K N°23 Porsche KG Salzburg Technique. Author ZANTAFIO56, File:24 heures du Mans 1970 (5001255204).jpg - Wikimedia Commons, 14 June 1970, Creative Commons Attribution 2.0 Generic license.

Photo 41 Matra: Matra Simca MS 670 N°15 Equipe Matra Simca Shell Technique. Author ZANTAFIO56, File:24H du Mans 1972 (5074896897).jpg - Wikimedia Commons, 11 June 1972, Creative Commons Attribution 2.0 Generic license.

Porsche Dominance: 1980 – 1989

Photo 42 1982 Porsche: Porsche 956 #2 - Jochen Mass & Vern Schuppan approaches the Esses at Le Mans 1982. Author Martin Lee, File:Porsche 956 -2 - Jochen Mass & Vern Schuppan approaches the Esses at Le Mans 1982 (50083051177).jpg - Wikimedia Commons, 7 January 2008, Creative Commons Attribution 2.0 Generic license.

Group C and LMGT1: 1990 – 1999

Photo 43 Mazda 1991: 1991 24 Hours of Le Mans, Mazda 787B. Author JPRoche, File:Le Mans-120121-0073FP.jpg - Wikimedia Commons, 21 January 2012, Creative Commons Attribution-Share Alike 3.0 license.

Photo 44 1995 McLaren: Ferrari F40GTE and Mclaren F1 GTR train through the Esses at Le Mans 1995. Author Martin Lee, File:Ferrari F40GTE and Mclaren F1 GTR train through the Esses at Le Mans 1995 (49627174896).jpg - Wikimedia Commons, 4 March 2020, Creative Commons Attribution 2.0 Generic license.

Photo 45 1998: Nissan R390 GT1 - Kazuyoshi Hoshino, Aguri Suzuki & Masahiko Kageyama chases Nissan R390 GT1 - Masami Kageyama, Satoshi Motoyama & Takuya Kurosawa across the finish line at the 1998 Le Mans. Author Martin Lee, File:Nissan R390 GT1 - Kazuyoshi Hoshino, Aguri Suzuki & Masahiko Kageyama chases Nissan R390 GT1 - Masami Kageyama, Satoshi Motoyama & Takuya Kurosawa across the finish line at the 1998 Le Mans (51885198251).jpg - Wikimedia Commons, 4 February 2022, Creative Commons Attribution 2.0 Generic license.

Photo 46 1998 Porsche: Porsche 911 GT1 - Jorg Muller, Uwe Alzen & Bob Wollek head under the Dunlop Bridge at the 1998 Le Mans. Author Martin Lee, File:Porsche 911 GT1 - Jorg Muller, Uwe Alzen & Bob Wollek head under the Dunlop Bridge at the 1998 Le Mans (51885183568).jpg - Wikimedia Commons, 3 February 2022, Creative Commons Attribution 2.0 Generic license.

Photo 47 1999 BMW: TOP: The winning BMW V12 LMR - Pierluigi Martini, Yannick Dalmas & Joachim Winkelhock at Ford Chicane at the 1999 Le Mans. Author Martin Lee, File:The winning BMW V12 LMR - Pierluigo Martini, Yannick Dalmas & Joachim Winkelhock at the 1999 Le Mans (51970869186).jpg - Wikimedia Commons. File:The winning BMW V12 LMR - Pierluigi Martini, Yannick Dalmas & Joachim Winkelhock at Ford Chicane at the 1999 Le Mans (51910306285).jpg - Wikimedia Commons. Creative Commons Attribution 2.0 Generic license.

The Science

Photo 48 Science cover (full page background picture): artwork by David Taylor

LMP1: 2000 – 2009

Photo 49 2003 Bentley: The winning Bentley Speed 8 - Rinaldo Capello, Tom Kristensen & Guy Smith at the Esses during the 2003 Le Mans. Author Martin Lee, File:The winning Bentley Speed 8 - Rinaldo Capello, Tom Kristensen & Guy Smith at the Esses during the 2003 Le Mans (28298656368).jpg - Wikimedia Commons, 23 June 2003, Creative Commons Attribution 2.0 Generic license.

Photo 50 2009: Le Mans 2009. Author David Merrett, File:Peugeot 908 and Oreca.jpg - Wikimedia Commons, 13 June 2009, Creative Commons Attribution 2.0 Generic license.

Le Mans on the Silver Screen

Photo 51 Le Mans Silver screen: artwork by David Taylor

Photo 52 Truth in 24 II: Le Mans 2011 - Race - Audi R18 TDI #2 and Peugeot 908 #8 and #7 in the Esses. Author Alessandro Prada, File:2011 Le Mans 24 Race 01.jpg - Wikimedia Commons, 12 June 2011, Creative Commons Attribution 2.0 Generic license.

Photo 53 Journey to Le Mans: Charlotte Fantelli Journey to Le Mans premiere, Vue cinema Leicester Square. Author Steve Burton, File:Charlotte-Fantelli-Journey-to-le-mans-premiere. jpg - Wikimedia Commons, Creative Commons Attribution 3.0 Generic license.

Jota Sport

Photo 54 Jota 2022: The Oreca 07 that won the 2022 24 Hours of Le Mans in the LMP2 class. Author ACBE25, File:Jota38LM2022.jpg - Wikimedia Commons, 12 June 2022, Creative Commons Attribution 4.0 Generic license.

Photo 55 Jota 2015: La Gibson 015S. Author Alain Janssoone, File:Gibson 015S - Nissan - Jota Sport - 24 Hours of Le Mans 2015.jpg - Wikimedia Commons, 10 June 2015, Creative Commons Attribution 2.5 Generic license.

The Hybrid Era: 2010 – 2020

Photo 56 2010 Finish: Finish. Mike Rockenfeller (#9), Benoît Tréluyer (#8) and Rinaldo Capello (#7). Author Arnaud333, File:Lemans-20100613-final.jpg - Wikimedia Commons, 13 June 2010, Creative Commons Attribution 3.0 Generic license.

Photo 57 2014 start: The Start The #7 Toyota crosses the line as Fernando Alonso drops the flag to commence the 2014 24 Hours of Le Mans. Author Nic Redhead, File:Le Mans Start 2014.jpg - Wikimedia Commons, 14 June 2014, Creative Commons Attribution 2.0 Generic license.

Ken Miles: The best driver never to win Le Mans?

Photo 58 Ken Miles Le Mans 1966: 1966 24 Hours of Le Mans. Author ZANTAFIO56, File:1966 24 Hours of Le Mans 1 (4771000677).jpg - Wikimedia Commons, June 1966, Creative Commons Attribution 2.0 Generic license.

Constructors with the most wins of all time

Photo 59 Toyota: Toyota GT-One - Keiichi Tsuchiya, Ukyou Katayama & Toshio Suzuki in the Esses at the 1998 Le Mans. Author Martin Lee, File:Toyota GT-One - Keiichi Tsuchiya, Ukyou Katayama & Toshio Suzuki in the Esses at the 1998 Le Mans (51860443244).jpg - Wikimedia Commons, 31 January 2022, Creative Commons Attribution 2.0 Generic license.

Photo 60 Matra: Matra Simca MS 670 N°15 Equipe Matra Simca Shell Technique. Author ZANTAFIO56, File:24H du Mans 1972 (5074965827).jpg - Wikimedia Commons, 11 June 1972, Creative Commons Attribution 2.0 Generic license.

Hypercar

Photo 61 Hypercar (full page background picture): Porsche 963 in Daytona test. Author Conor 27m, File:Porsche-963-lmdh-1.jpg - Wikimedia Commons, 9 December 2022, Creative Commons Attribution 4.0 Generic license.

Photo 62 Glickenhaus: The #708 Glickenhaus Racing SCG 007 LMH at the 2021 24 Hours of Le Mans. Author Kobokem2021, File:2021 24 Hours of Le Mans Scuderia Cameron Glickenhaus Glickenhaus SCG 007 LMH.jpg - Wikimedia Commons, 18 August 2021, Creative Commons Attribution 4.0 Generic license.

Photo 63 Porsche 963: 2023 Super Sebring. Author Rick Flores, File:Porsche 963 Sebring 2023.jpg - Wikimedia Commons, 18 March 2023, Creative Commons Attribution 2.0 Generic license.

Records and Stats
Photo 64 Dunlop Bridge: KAM_3489. Author kevinmcgill, File:KAM 3489 (9120934054).jpg - Wikimedia Commons, 20 June 2013, Creative Commons Attribution 2.0 Generic license.

Every effort has been made to acknowledge correctly the source, author, and licences of each picture. Any unintentional errors or omissions will be corrected in future editions of this book.

Ingram Content Group UK Ltd.
Milton Keynes UK
UKHW050610010623
422698UK00009B/46